Quarterly Essay

Quarterly Essay is published four times a year by Black Inc., an imprint of Schwartz Publishing Pty Ltd. Publisher: Morry Schwartz.

ISBN 978-1-86395-786-1 ISSN 1832-0953

Subscriptions – 1 year print & digital (4 issues): $79.95 within Australia incl. GST. Outside Australia $119.95. 2 years print & digital (8 issues): $129.95 within Australia incl. GST. 1 year digital only: $39.95.

Payment may be made by Mastercard or Visa, or by cheque made out to Schwartz Publishing. Payment includes postage and handling.

To subscribe, fill out and post the subscription card or form inside this issue, or subscribe online:

www.quarterlyessay.com
subscribe@blackincbooks.com
Phone: 61 3 9486 0288

Correspondence should be addressed to:

The Editor, Quarterly Essay
37–39 Langridge Street
Collingwood VIC 3066 Australia
Phone: 61 3 9486 0288 / Fax: 61 3 9486 0244
Email: quarterlyessay@blackincbooks.com

Editor: Chris Feik. Management: Sophy Williams, Caitlin Yates. Publicity: Anna Lensky. Design: Guy Mirabella. Assistant Editor: Kirstie Innes-Will. Production Coordinator: Siân Scott-Clash. Typesetting: Duncan Blachford.

Printed by Griffin Press, Australia. The paper used to produce this book comes from wood grown in sustainable forests.

POLITICAL
AMNESIA | How *We* Forgot How to Govern

Laura Tingle

THE DANGEROUS PAST

June 2015. Clouds are scudding across a pale, bright winter sky on the road from Sydney to Canberra as the fall of the Roman Republic unfolds before me. The small girl I described at the beginning of my 2012 Quarterly Essay, *Great Expectations* – having her picture taken in front of the Pantheon in Rome in 2009 – is now sixteen and fretting about a looming Ancient History exam as we travel through a landscape of silvery gums and naked poplar trees.

The collapse of Rome's second triumvirate – Octavian, Mark Antony and Lepidus – and the beginnings of the Empire have featured heavily in our lives over the last few weeks, enriched by reading the sources from which all knowledge of these events has come for the past 2000 years. "When after the destruction of Brutus and Cassius there was no longer any army of the Commonwealth," Tacitus (with his wonderful and rhythmic disdain for the full stop) wrote of Octavian's rise to become Emperor Augustus:

when Pompeius was crushed in Sicily, and when, with Lepidus pushed aside and Antonius slain, even the Julian faction had only Caesar left to lead it, then, dropping the title of triumvir, and giving out that he was a Consul, and was satisfied with a tribune's authority for the protection of the people, Augustus won over the soldiers with gifts, the populace with cheap corn, and all men with the sweets of repose, and so grew greater by degrees, while he concentrated in himself the functions of the Senate, the magistrates, and the laws. He was wholly unopposed, for the boldest spirits had fallen in battle, or in the proscription, while the remaining nobles, the readier they were to be slaves, were raised the higher by wealth and promotion, so that, aggrandised by revolution, they preferred the safety of the present to the dangerous past.

Tell me the story from the beginning, I say to our daughter, Tosca. Saying it out loud often helps clarify how it all fits together. Tosca starts the story with Julius Caesar's birth in 100 BC, punctuates it with teenage idiom and endures my hilarious attempts to cast contemporary politicians and events as players in the drama. Layers and layers of history pile up: the Senate, the *Optimates* and *Populares*, the returning legions who have been promised land, the tax collectors, the Rubicon, the marriages, ambition, human weakness, political cunning and intrigue which shape the events that affect the lives of countless people across Rome's domains.

All of us know at least something of ancient Rome, whether from a cursory high-school glance, from Shakespeare, from a 1950s Hollywood swords-and-sandals epic or from reading the classics. Likewise, all of us know at least something of our recent political history. The "dangerous past" of which Tacitus spoke – whether it be events two thousand, twenty or even two years ago – gives us the conscious, but often unconscious, context for our understanding of contemporary events.

Our first response to an unfolding political episode is often to go to our wardrobe of memories and see whether we can clothe the new incident in one of the dramas of the past, or see how it fits into the pattern of our recollections. Malcolm Turnbull's strike against Tony Abbott in September 2015 was overwhelmingly portrayed in the language and clichés of Julia Gillard's coup against Kevin Rudd in 2010. It was a "late-night coup." There were "faceless men," and Australians were going to bed with one prime minister and waking up with another.

Upon winning government in 2013, Tony Abbott and his colleagues referred back to their memories of the political strategy that worked for Prime Minister John Howard. Bill Shorten and his colleagues – all too young to have been close to the workings of the Hawke–Keating government – conjure up a ghostly memory of policy glory as a backdrop, and in this way stake a claim to credibility for their own policies. Journalists confronting the day-to-day dramas of politics draw comparisons with previous events, whether these be leadership coups or policy brawls.

There are hazards in trying to jam current events into the mould of past experience. We are so busy looking for, or assuming, similarities that we often miss the fact that it is the peculiar differences which most define the present episode. But even more dangerous than a confused and jumbled memory of the past is no memory at all.

This essay is about the role of memory in politics and policy-making in Australia. It is about the dangers of having little, if any, memory of what has gone before. It is about the collapse of the institutions that once formed a safe archive of these memories. I argue that a powerful reason our politics has become not only inane and ugly but dangerous is our growing political and policy amnesia. In *Great Expectations* I argued that one of the reasons for our national anger was that people no longer knew what they wanted from, or could expect of, government. Our politicians still speak in the language and play to a set of expectations formed at a time when our economy was heavily regulated. Politicians once had the power to set interest rates and the exchange rate, and to protect industries from overseas competition. There were mechanisms in place to set wage rates for the whole country. That all changed with the deregulation of the economy that began in the 1980s. But politics did not. Politicians still promise, or else imply, that they can control events when they cannot. This essay takes a different tack in considering a question that leaves so many of us perplexed: why is our politics unable to deal with the pressing issues of the country? Surely it cannot simply be that the current generation of politicians are a bunch of duds?

Tacitus tells us that the Romans preferred the "safety of the present" to what he clearly thinks was a better, republican past. Yearning for such a past became a dangerous sentiment when Augustus had concentrated the powers of the state in his own hands, silenced those who had spoken against his rise to power, and bribed the rest with gifts, and cheap corn, and the "sweets of repose." It was easier, Tacitus suggests, to forget.

In Australia today, we have a different dilemma. At a time when people are not just angry about politics but befuddled by the way our institutions – and our presumptions about legal rights and freedoms – are under challenge, there is a yearning for the past – a less dangerous past. We yearn for a time when politics appeared to be conducted in the national interest, when government policy was well developed and thoroughly thought through, and when the media were less shrill and gave us an informed context for assessing events.

Much is said about the dumbing-down of politics; the 24-hour news cycle; too much polling and poll-driven politics; the decline of community involvement in political organisations; the rise of the political professional; and the decline of "real-life" experience among our politicians. Without doubt, these all play a role. But elements that I think are regularly overlooked are more fundamental: the role of memory and the changing nature of risk-taking in politics. I argue that there is a growing loss of institutional memory about *how* things have come about, and, more importantly perhaps, *why* they did.

Without memory, there is no context or continuity for the making of new decisions. We have little choice but to take these decisions at face value, as the inevitable outcome of current circumstance. The perils of this are manifest. Decisions are taken that are not informed by knowledge of what has worked, or not worked, in the past, or even by a conscious analysis of what might have changed since the issue was last considered.

This thought first struck me a few years ago during the Gillard government's wild ride through office. In 2012 child care suddenly became the issue of the day. The prime minister called an "emergency child-care summit." One of the proposals floated as an answer to the problems in child care was to shift government subsidies from parents to providers. For twenty-four hours there was much learned discussion in the media of the pros and cons of this idea, as if it were an entirely new shiny thing. I watched on, puzzled. "Am I the only person," I asked a senior public servant, "who remembers that this is the way child care used to be funded?" "Probably," was his sardonic reply.

Some might believe that stripping an issue of the baggage of the past makes analysis more straightforward: the matter at hand can be seen more clearly in the light of present circumstances. I would say, "No." Instead, it is more likely to become the victim of oversimplified slogans and ideological conclusions. The scope for there to be nuance, or "grey," in discussion of an issue instead of black and white disappears, and with it the capacity for compromise. Rational debate about the pros and cons of an issue becomes too hard for both advocates and audience. We slip into the habit of conducting our debates in the present tense.

Consider two of the great issues of the past decade: climate change and national security. Climate change moved from being a debate about the implications of scientific findings developed over a couple of decades to a paranoid debate replete with conspiracy theories and anti-science. It moved from a debate about the pros and cons of different market mechanisms to reduce carbon emissions to a debate about whether one such mechanism is a tax or not. Such simplification robs the issue of its context, its own history. Participants are not required to address all of the questions that surround the issue, informed by the history of the contributions to the debate until now.

National security. Well, who can argue with national security? Few in politics dare to raise doubts or scruples these days, for fear of being dubbed traitorous. We have got out of the habit of discussing our foreign and strategic policy as part of mainstream public debate. That has robbed us of the confidence of historical knowledge – or even a decent contemporary knowledge – to assess and argue the present-day case. Terrorism has added a new layer to the national security debate. Unlike the hulk and bulk of traditional defence, it has the advantage of being everywhere and nowhere. Our enemies, and their methods, are morphing all the time. Terrorism is presented as something totally new, different to everything that has gone before, and therefore not able to be assessed in historical frameworks. To this is added a rationale for why we can't be told what is going on in the work of securing our community. We have to just pay the amount – both in taxpayer dollars and surrendered freedoms – that national security requires us to pay. We just have to believe what we are told.

It's not just the internal workings of the spy agencies. Executive decisions are taken which fundamentally change our relationships with our major allies and trading partners – the United States, Japan and China – without warning being given to the public at large. Since the end of the Cold War, there has not really been a sophisticated and ongoing national political debate about Australia's strategic interests in the wider world, and our place in it. As a result, few apart from the specialists are prepared to enter the policy fray with any confidence. When politicians do venture to raise such issues in mainstream debate, we often enter the realm of shrill panic and knee-jerk reactions. I believe this has helped to stoke a growing insularity. And we also see the incremental creep of the national security mindset into other issues that are just "too hard," such as how we deal with asylum seekers.

Political amnesia also plays out in perplexing ways in the actions of politicians. For example, there is the baffling question of how the Abbott government could apparently repeat, almost move for move, all the political and policy mistakes of the Labor government, even though these mistakes were less than five years old, even though the senior members of the Abbott government were there to watch those mistakes, and learnt to profit from them in Opposition. The joke in both Labor and Coalition ranks, before things became so grim they were no longer funny, was that the Abbott government had stolen Labor's book about mistakes and was systematically going through it, ticking off every disaster. There is the equally perplexing question of how so many senior members of the current government managed to live through the Howard years – some as cabinet ministers – and yet not absorb any lessons of how government works, or how to go about making things happen.

This world of foggy memories – and mediocre politics – has often helped take us back to the political equivalent of debating science versus religion. It has cleared the way for a vapid politics of three-word slogans and the "cheap corn" of appealing to our basest instincts and self-interest. It has cleared the way for us to find ourselves on a shifting battlefield of fairly ugly ideology rather than "evidence-based" politics and policy.

It is telling that Malcolm Turnbull's claim to return to the Coalition leadership in 2015 was so heavily based on a recognition that the lessons of good government – and good politics – have been forgotten, and on the need to restore the processes and institutions that help enshrine them. We are about to find out whether his memory is good enough to transport us out of the political wilderness in which we find ourselves.

*

Some might argue that an ideological, quasi-religious tone to our politics is hardly new. For the past thirty years, the overwhelming dogma when it came to the future of government has been what was once called "economic rationalism." It long ago became taken for granted in politics – and in the broader political debate – that market-driven outcomes are always the best. Similarly, the presumption is that the private sector knows how to do things better than the public sector, and that governments in general are bad. All sorts of public policy has been built on these foundations:

government debt is always bad; contracting out is good; the public sector should adopt the managerialism and language of the private sector; public assets should be privatised; government regulation is little more than a frustrating pile of red tape.

To argue against these propositions, particularly at the height of the fervour in the 1980s and '90s, was to invite ridicule or contempt. Groups representing poor people – and arguing to government about the impact of policies affecting them – had to commission economic modelling to demonstrate this impact on incentives to work, efficient outcomes and national productivity if they were to have any chance of a hearing.

And of course it affected the way politics was conducted. At the beginning, at least, the "economic rationalist" push was about understanding and confronting the systems of protection that had been at work in the economy since federation, and identifying their beneficiaries and quantifying their cost to everyone else. There was a pent-up pressure to confront the distortions being caused by our protectionist economy in a world that was changing dramatically as oil prices soared and international exchange-rate mechanisms collapsed. Arguments had numbers and details attached to them. Advocates took satisfaction in creating policy structures that worked seamlessly in several different ways to create better outcomes.

However, this obligation to explain and advocate has been supplanted by a form of political shorthand over the years. Politicians and policy advocates now say "reform" and hope that it conjures up all that earlier work, that earlier "consensus" on change. Saying "reform" of itself, however, does not mean the policy being produced is of the same quality, that it is doing the same job, has the same aims, or even recognises that times have moved on. "Reform" has become a hollowed-out word which you attach to anything you think voters won't like in the hope that it will make you appear a strong and decisive government. Nobody ever takes a decision in government to cut spending, or increase spending, or raise or lower taxes anymore. They "do reform."

The focus on reducing budget deficits has not only meant a perpetual search for savings and greater efficiencies, but also a gradual shift in the way anything done by the public sector is perceived. The head of Victoria's Department of Health and Human Services, Pradeep Philip, noted in a recent speech that "seeing health, education, social services as being a 'drag' or 'drain' on the economy or on the budget" has become very popular in our public debate and policy practice. He concluded:

> These areas are seen as parasitic on – rather than contributing to – overall economic performance. This notion of the priority of the economic and the subservience of a parasitic social policy is simply wrong as a way of thinking about public policy.

*

In 1982 the then secretary to the Treasury, John Stone, famously dismissed as "meretricious players" policy advisers from outside the public service in political offices. His comments, in what was supposedly a private letter to a business magazine, were seen as a particular swipe at John Hewson, then economic adviser in the office of the treasurer in the Fraser government, John Howard. "Public servants," Stone wrote:

> perhaps because they have a continuing responsibility to provide advice and to stay on and live with its consequences – have longer memories than the more meretricious players who flit across the private ministerial advisory stage.

The problem we have now is that public servants don't necessarily stay on and live with the consequences of policy decisions. They don't necessarily have longer memories. Stone was among the last of the powerful mandarins in Canberra who, like *Yes Minister*'s Sir Humphrey Appleby, not only ran the place a good deal of the time, but were also firmly of the view that the public service provided stability for the country while the politicians came and went.

There has been much said over the years since John Stone reigned at Treasury about the politicisation of the public service. But less has been said about the more complex set of changes that have flowed from the "privatising" of the public sector, whether through the actual contracting out of service delivery, the rise of the political adviser or the attempts to import private-sector managerialism into the sector. In general, the push against government intervention and delivery of services by the public sector, and for contestability in all things, has had a little-recognised but devastating effect. I argue that these changes have largely left the public service without an institutional memory of its own, and, as a result, with neither its power base nor the capacity to provide a ballast to short-term politics.

The periodic mass axing of public service heads upon the arrival of incoming conservative governments has created a caution in the culture. The bureaucracy has been cowed both by the prospect of being sacked and by a reward system which punishes taking risks.

But just as important has been the loss of memory associated with the managerial changes of the past three decades. Increased opportunities – particularly for economists – in the private sector have robbed the public sector of many of the brightest minds it might have once claimed. Other changes have been eating away more insidiously. For example, ambitious public servants will tell you that the best path to promotion is to switch regularly between departments rather than stay in the one place, meaning no one develops deep expertise in anything, with just a few exceptions, such as defence, national security and foreign affairs. Bureaucrats going for a promotion are more likely to be assessed on the strength of how they have managed service-delivery contracts than on, for example, their institutional memory of the history of child-care policy and what worked or didn't.

Equally, going outside a policy department to get the best private-sector experts in a field to consider an issue has a lot going for it. However, it also means the department never gets the opportunity to develop that expertise itself. Contracting out the delivery of services to private-sector or non-government agency providers might suggest one will get better value for money. But it also means that not only does the public no longer know whether those services are being properly delivered, nor do the public servants responsible for their delivery.

It is therefore no longer the case that public servants have longer memories than the meretricious players. And without memories, their capacity, their gravitas to advise politicians, is diminished or wiped out. Some senior public servants I have spoken to for this essay doubt that large swathes of the public service actually have the capacity, or memory, to provide policy advice to their political masters anymore, should it be requested. One of John Stone's successors as secretary to the Treasury, Ken Henry, says simply: "I think many departments have lost the capacity to develop policy; but not just that, they have lost their memory. I seriously doubt there is any serious policy development going on in most government departments." Martin Parkinson, who followed Henry as Treasury secretary, believes there has been an erosion of institutions, of both their independence and capability:

> The blurring of boundaries between the public servant and the political adviser, and the relentless focus on message over substance, results in a diminution of the "space" in which the independent adviser can operate. Becoming an effective policy adviser also requires "learning by doing" under the guidance of experienced hands – an apprenticeship, if you will. Today, in some institutions, smart people look around at their colleagues and find there is no one to talk to, to learn from, who has experience in delivering real reform. The combination of these two things is a decline in the quality of advice and an erosion of capability, to the detriment of good government.

The loss of memory has been drastically exacerbated by the big redundancy rounds of the past few years under both Labor and the Coalition.

Older public servants – the ones with the longest memories – have often comprised the majority of the departures.

If public servants are asked how policies they oversee are being implemented, they are also constrained in their answers by the fact that the implementation is now being done by contractors, or even contractors to contractors. The lines of responsibility, accountability and reporting are not good.

The point here is not to suggest that market-driven outcomes were, or were not, always the best; that the private sector does, or doesn't, know how to do things better than the public sector; that governments in general are, or are not, all bad. It is to observe that, in practice, some of these changes have not been good; that they have had many destructive side effects. Yet we have not at any point stopped to look back and frankly assess what has been good and what has been bad, and whether we need to change not just policy but the way we think about entire issues, and how we think about the role of the public sector.

Think of how events at Australia's detention centre on Manus Island unfolded last year, leading to the death of one young man. And how we had a lot of trouble finding out what had occurred, because of the complex set of contracts in place to manage the centre. Would we accept a regime where people acting in our name are jailed for talking about what is happening on Manus Island quite so easily if they were public servants, rather than contractors, and therefore so much more obviously acting in our name?

Think of how so much that was criticised during the Rudd government's response to the global economic crisis came back to the fact that the government had so little real control over what occurred, whether in the school-building program or the home-insulation program, because the federal government simply doesn't do such things directly anymore.

Think of how utter horror at the idea of government voluntarily taking on any debt – for any purpose – has helped produce Australia's disgraceful lack of physical infrastructure, despite the largest economic boom in our history.

*

"Reform" may continue as a fetish word, but the lust for economic reform, its centrality in the political debate, started to fade in the Howard years. John Howard came into office in 1996 with a couple of new constructs to shape the political agenda. His attack and potency was not on economics but on a culture he derided as "political correctness," which was embodied in Labor's social (not economic) policies. Reflecting both a growing revolt in some parts of the electorate, and a frustration at the dominance of Labor culture in conservative circles, Howard argued that a "political correctness" was at work in Australia which didn't allow ordinary Australians to express their disquiet over welfare recipients or Asian immigration or Aboriginal people. Australia was being run by "elites" whose opinions didn't reflect those of the "mainstream" or "silent majority." Conservative commentators, with no sense of irony, complained about the "chattering classes."

But just as economic rationalism first changed the economic debate and then hollowed it out, Howard's push back against what he saw as a self-censoring Australian political discussion had its own fallout. It gave room for people like Pauline Hanson to emerge. There was a new intolerance for those advocating for asylum seekers, or indigenous people, or the marginalised. Such advocates were characterised as "bleeding hearts," or in more recent years the ultimate insult: "lefties." It seems there is no one in the middle ground anymore. You are either a "mainstream Australian" or a "leftie."

The new political correctness has been fuelled by the morphing of Rupert Murdoch's Australian media into something more closely reflecting that of his British and American operations. In the post-Watergate period there had been a general delusion that while media proprietors might have clear political biases, their newspapers reported events as papers of record, and that the media have a role to play in holding politicians to account. But then the media went tabloid and became ideologically divided and shrill (as they often have been in the past). The astonishing speed of the rise of social media as a platform for news increased the chances that voters could choose to hear news only through the filter of their own prejudices, whether of the "left" or "right." In such an environment, history and memory are no longer anchors but selectively chosen and lethal weapons.

This ideological division and the capacity to filter what you want to hear has only made worse the loss of institutional memory that the changing media landscape has fuelled. The web and the electronic news cycle means we are perpetually looking forward to the next bit of the story, never pausing to consider where it has come from, and whether we have been here before.

History and memory have long been the plaything of politicians, myth-makers and propagandists. There is a rich academic literature on the politics of memory, mostly associated with memories of war. And Tacitus and Shakespeare are part of a long tradition of using history to frame more modern politics and collective memory. But the spectacular boldness and the almost instantaneous rewriting of history that seem to be part of a frenzied national debate these days are reasonably new in Australia. Without the ballast of any sense of continuity, and without the anchor of a strong "push-back" against political whim, politics and policy have spun down into a series of reactions and counter-reactions that play out in vacuous daily news grabs and zingers. It is an opportunity for the politically adroit, and the philosophically bankrupt, to exploit.

No essay on the role of memory in politics would be complete without the famous words of Spanish-American philosopher George Santayana, who said in 1905:

> Progress, far from consisting in change, depends on retentiveness. When change is absolute there remains no being to improve and no direction is set for possible improvement: and when experience is

not retained, as among savages, infancy is perpetual. Those who cannot remember the past are condemned to repeat it.

Santayana said something else pretty important too:

Fanaticism consists in redoubling your efforts when you have forgotten your aim.

From where I sit, that is how our political discourse feels: the banging on a hollow vessel that comes when you repeat something so often that you can't remember why you were saying it in the first place. There are big, dangerous questions that flow from these observations. Can we fix it? Where does it lead us if we don't? How is power in our society, as well as our discourse, being rebalanced by these profound changes in our institutional structures?

Malcolm Turnbull's pitch for the prime ministership rested on his pledge to fix what is wrong with the way government works. The fact that so many of the key institutions in our society are suffering their own interlinked but different lapses in memory makes that hard, and leads to shoulder-shrugging and head-shaking about how bad things are.

What to do? Nothing is impossible to change. But first we must understand how it has come about.

John Phillips, a tall, angular, still man who wore his double-breasted suits with a style that always seemed to speak of another age, joined the Commonwealth Bank from school in January 1946. He worked as a teller in a city branch in Sydney. When the Commonwealth Bank was split in 1960 into two very separate operations – commercial and central – Phillips went to the new Reserve Bank and became a central banker. In the days before the floating of the dollar, if you wanted to buy or sell Australian dollars in exchange for foreign currency, you had to buy them from, or sell them to, John Phillips. Phillips sat on the committee of Treasury and Reserve Bank officials that, each morning, set the exchange rate for the Australian dollar, and in so doing set the most important price in the economy, one that had knock-on effects for every other price, including wages. He left the bank in 1992 as deputy governor – having earned the displeasure of Paul Keating for daring to contradict government mantra on economic policy – for a new and successful life as a company director. But he continued to serve the public as the chair of the Foreign Investment Review Board from 1997 until 2012 – just two years before his death – sixty-six years after his career had begun as a fifteen-year-old.

The huge Sydney funeral for John Phillips in 2014 was held in the same week as the state memorial service for Gough Whitlam. The two men represented links, of different sorts, back through the history of post-war Australian policy-making and a changing relationship between politicians and the public service. Whitlam had grown up at the very centre of the new federal government machinery in Canberra as the child of the solicitor-general. As prime minister, however, he started the rupture of the cosy and trusting relationship between politicians and the public service that had begun after World War II, survived the change of government from Labor to Liberal in 1949, and run the country through the sleepy prosperity of the Menzies years. John Phillips had an institutional memory of Australian monetary policy – and economic policy more broadly – going back half a century.

Ironically, perhaps, the very institution where Phillips spent so much of his life – the Reserve Bank – has been far less affected by the changes I will discuss here, because central bank independence – bestowed by politicians – has made the bank largely immune to them. As a result, it serves as a living reminder of what happens when you don't stuff up the public sector. It has maintained its institutional memory, a clear sense of purpose and the capacity both to develop and to rethink policy.

There has been much talk in the past thirty years about the politicisation of the public service and the rise of the ministerial adviser. But what has happened to the public service – and as a result to the quality of our policy-making – is a much more complex story than mere politicisation. We once scoffed at the Sir Humphrey-esque world of the senior mandarins of the public service, so out of touch with the real world, whose apparent view was that they were the ones really running the country, if only those wretched politicians who came and went would stop interfering. But I fear we have lost more than a caricature over the past thirty years. We have not just lost frank and fearless advice; we have lost the memory of how policy has been made before, of the history of the groups and issues with which government must interact every day. Government in the broader sense of the word, therefore, has lost much of its capacity to remember and thus to learn from past mistakes.

Deregulation of the economy unleashed a process of structural change to what the public sector does, and how it interacts with the rest of Australia. Much of the change was well-intentioned and, indeed, necessary. But some of it, sometimes unwittingly, has been destructive of the public sector – and it is only beginning to dawn on people just how destructive. The changes of the past thirty years have left us largely bereft of an institutional memory of government policy, let alone a memory of how relationships between politicians and the public service could be different. Yet the speed of political debate means the need for that working memory has never been more important.

To understand what has happened, we need to go back to the period from 1945 to 1972, which saw the rise of a public service culture encapsulated in the legend of a group of civil servants known as the Seven Dwarfs. As Nicholas Brown notes in his book *The Seven Dwarfs and the Age of the Mandarins*, they were "'the new mandarins' – a wider company of senior bureaucrats – who rose to prominence in that period, and were associated with a distinct ethic of independence and authority." Brown notes that who exactly the Seven Dwarfs were ended up being a debate moderated by the *Australian Dictionary of Biography* – the list always included Sir Roland Wilson, Nugget Coombs and Sir John Crawford, but there were many others. The reality was that it was a great name to give a small group of sometimes stature-challenged public servants. Brown writes:

> The seven dwarfs symbolise the transformation of government under the pressures of the Second World War ... This element is exemplified by the Keynesian paradigm: government transformed by young, university-trained, and theoretically informed reformers. These figures sought to translate a broad domain of civic concern formed in contexts of depression and unemployment into careers spent dealing with pressures first of wartime mobilisation and reconstruction, then of inflation and full employment, and with the expanding role of public investment in general.

Brown says these men "were emphatically not the economic rationalists of the 1980s, with their deference to the discipline of the market. They were instead conscious – as Coombs would put it – of using 'other people's money' to achieve a range of social outcomes within the context of a tight bargain between stability and growth, prosperity and regulation, the respective roles and responsibilities of the government and the people."

Whatever they were trying to achieve, the Seven Dwarfs' influence was as much about human relationships as it was about the role of government.

Don Russell, a former Treasury officer and chief of staff to Paul Keating as treasurer and prime minister, observed in a 2014 speech that:

> The Prime Minister of the day and the Prime Minister's Office spend a very large amount of their time managing individual Ministers and dealing with their problems. Using a cricket analogy, Chifley spoke of the long tail of the batting line up of his Ministerial colleagues; Menzies too had doubts about the calibre of his Cabinet. Having a diversity of talent in the Cabinet is not necessarily a bad thing but it needs to be managed. Chifley liked to be surrounded by clever people who could do things; the post WWII elite of Secretaries in Canberra [that is, the Seven Dwarfs] was the result. Menzies inherited Chifley's public service. To Menzies it was preferable to have power in Canberra tied up in the hands of a senior cadre of talented high officials answerable to him than to have it dissipated through a collection of Ministers for whom he had only modest regard.

Russell argues, however, that the next generation of secretaries – by which he means the generation that had reached the zenith of its power in the 1960s and early 1970s – "misunderstood the basis of their power and overreached." This produced a bipartisan consensus among politicians that "the policy agenda should belong with Ministers; that they should be equipped to develop policy proposals; and they should no longer be hostage to powerful officials dictating what was and what was not acceptable."

When he came to office in 1972, Gough Whitlam began the process of challenging the all-powerful mandarins by introducing policy advisers into ministers' offices – a move reflecting Labor's suspicion of the public service after twenty-three years of Coalition government. "The Prime Minister giveth, and the Prime Minister taketh away," Russell says. "Advisers with policy responsibilities in all Ministers' Offices were the result. Ministerial advisers strengthen Ministers and can perform a very useful role working cooperatively with officials to make sure that the Minister makes the best use of the department, but they have changed the way Canberra operates."

The practical implications of this change go something like this: policy proposals would once have been largely developed by departments. Policy might be anything from how you pay unemployed people to the government's position on building a road, imposing taxes or going to war. A minister would have asked the department to tell him (in those days) how to go about putting an idea he, or the government, had about policy into action. Alternatively, a department might independently identify an issue that had arisen and put up a proposal to a minister. Before it went to cabinet, the department/minister's proposal would have been circulated to other departments for debate and input. There would be further debate in the "coordination comments" of departments when the matter got to the stage of a cabinet submission. The discussion would consider the pros and cons of proceeding with a particular idea, including its budgetary cost but also its positive and negative impacts on other groups. There would be data and summaries of what stakeholders thought about it. Much of this work was done by the "line" departments – the departments with direct responsibility for areas such as social welfare, health, resources and industry. The "central agencies" – Treasury (and later Finance) and Prime Minister and Cabinet (PM&C) – were responsible for providing advice on the implications of these policies from a "whole of government" perspective.

The department was the minister's main source of detailed advice about a policy area. There were experts in particular areas – health, say, or the aged pension. But there were also experts in other departments who had slightly different briefs to consider and whose expertise could be brought into the discussion. An example might be the crossover of perspectives on agriculture, environment, foreign investment and resources in the coal-seam gas extraction debate. The rise of the ministerial adviser not only meant that there were now alternative sources of advice, but that ministers would, increasingly, "work up" proposals that departments were cut out of, or would be asked to comment on, or provide supporting material for, only at the last moment.

Ministerial advisers – who increasingly did not come from a public service background, but were often faithful servants of the party that was forming government – might have limited expertise in making or executing policy, but a particularly political, or ideological, perspective. From the Hawke government onwards, legislative change gave advisers in ministerial offices a clearly defined, separate and much more flexible role than that of their public service colleagues. Bureaucrats – even working in a minister's office – had constraints placed on the tasks they could do, designed to ensure that they did not get involved in working on party-political matters.

As one long-serving bureaucrat observes, "everyone thought the world would go back to 'normal' after Whitlam: that these presumptuous ministers who had astounded them by not just doing as they were told would disappear. Instead, Malcolm Fraser took exactly the same position." The suspicion of the bureaucracy was still there when Bob Hawke came to office in 1983. A detailed secret brief was prepared within Labor for the new prime minister on the bureaucrats then heading government departments, outlining their strengths and weaknesses, but also their likely political allegiance.

Crucially, though, Hawke insisted his ministers should have bureaucrats in their offices, specifically as chiefs of staff. It kept open the links with the public service in both directions. Ministers' offices understood the public service. The public service understood their ministers. The suspicion was reduced. The two arms of government were largely able to work successfully together. Paul Kelly tells in The End of Certainty how Paul Keating went into the Treasury after the 1983 election and said, "I want a strong Treasury. It's an important national institution." There was a two-way benefit:

> The situation was ripe for the development of the Keating–Treasury relationship which became central to the government's character.

> The Treasury's relations with the outgoing Fraser government had virtually collapsed ... It found in Keating a clever novice but fast learner who possessed both personal candour and Cabinet clout. The Treasury was sick of being beaten in Cabinet during the Fraser years. Now it had a minister who would restore its authority.

But the era when executive government and the bureaucracy still worked cooperatively – often with creative tension – to get policy outcomes that were both politically and practically successful ended in 1996, when John Howard won government and sacked a raft of department heads in what became known as his "Night of the Long Knives." This sent a shockwave through the public service and, in combination with a series of radical reforms to the public sector, accelerated a decline in its ability to make policy.

Ironically, perhaps, John Howard's most successful years coincided with the times when a former public servant, Arthur Sinodinos, was running his office. There were still bureaucrats seconded to, and even running, the offices of many of his senior ministers. But over Howard's time in office, there was an inexorable shift towards policy being developed and made in ministerial offices, not the public service. "We'll do the thinking, you just implement it," was how one senior bureaucrat described the Howard government's attitude in its later stages.

Public service sackings, the tendency to run policy from ministerial offices and just get departments to implement it, and an increased willingness to make public servants the subject of "show trials" in parliamentary committee hearings, gradually cowed much of the public service and helped build a toadying culture.

Tony Abbott's sacking in 2013 of more public servants, including the head of Treasury, because of their association with policies on climate change and asylum seekers, to which the Coalition was hostile, raised even more questions. One senior bureaucrat said after the sackings that he found himself at a loss to know how to respond to more junior officers when they observed that the clear message was that you shouldn't stick your head up for any policy assignments that might later become contentious. Instead of being a place to make your name, new policy papers and areas were now a killing zone, it seemed.

Yet the role of the public service in government has not changed just because of the way ministers and public servants relate to each other. What has complicated and changed the relationship over time are the structural and managerial shifts. Departmental secretary was once a permanent appointment, but in the 1980s this started to change. Instead of staying on as the head of a department, moving about was preferred. Instead of holding your job until you retired, you took a fixed-term appointment. There was a lot to be said for the changes, but there were also risks. Governments now had the ability to appoint the best person for the job, but they also had the ability to sack people if they didn't think they fitted a particular political mould, or even because of personality differences. Significantly, senior public servants were not necessarily appointed because of their policy expertise in a particular area. They might have absolutely no knowledge of the history of a policy and how it operated.

Private-sector management techniques also arrived in the public sector: all the jargon about organisational goals, KPIs, performance reviews and a focus on outputs. As a result, the public service historian John Nethercote says, "scientific management has given way to business management as the inspiration for new thinking on operations."

As the fashion for spending restraint and greater efficiency arrived, the public service restructured what it did to concentrate on its "core" functions. Work that was regarded as subsidiary or administrative was contracted out to others. It started with things like property maintenance, personnel and legal services, but eventually grew under the Howard government into the wholesale transfer of government service delivery to the private sector, first with services to the unemployed through the Job Network. (The idea that the federal government would engage in actually planning or delivering capital works had hit the dust years earlier as an early victim of the Hawke government's spending cuts. The days of the federal government building the Snowy Mountains Hydro-electric Scheme, or Tullamarine Airport, or the telephone network, or hospitals and schools in the territories were now well and truly over.) Some of the Howard-era change was reasonable, but quite a lot of it was spectacularly stupid. For example, the government announced it would sell off any government building that was not returning 15 per cent a year – a return most in the private sector could only dream of. Large swathes of government-owned offices were sold off, only to be rented back by government departments at rents that reflected (notoriously, in the case of the Department of Foreign Affairs and Trade) that the departments were working in purpose-built buildings that couldn't easily be traded for others. The Australian National Audit Office reported in 2001 that: "the Department of Foreign Affairs and Trade advised ... that the net lettable area had been re-measured and that the new owner had formally notified the Department that they were seeking a 38 per cent increase in the base rent for the ... building."

One of the great ironies of public service reform in the past three decades is that the push to "contract out" went most spectacularly wrong in the place where it should have been most at home: the Department of Finance. In a move partly aimed at reducing the power of the Treasury, Malcolm Fraser split it into two departments in the 1970s, leaving policy-making in Treasury but creating the new Department of Finance to monitor spending by the bureaucracy. In the following two decades, Finance developed an expertise in all the policy areas of government. Public servants – and politicians – will tell you that the portfolio experts in Finance in the 1980s and early 1990s – the people who kept tabs on health, education and defence spending, for example – knew more about how their portfolios worked than the departments that oversaw them. Finance knew where all the money was hidden or buried and how the mechanics of a policy worked, or didn't.

Of course, Finance notoriously also hated spending money. When the new broom swept through government after the 1996 election, it was Finance that grasped it most fervently. Perhaps believing in leading by example, Finance melted itself down. It was stripped of most of its experienced staff and, with them, its institutional memory. Finance bureaucrats went off to advise other governments around the world on how to set up governance systems. Some were hired back on vastly inflated contracts for specific jobs. But the core work of the department was gutted. "People walked out the door with the entire capital stock," one bureaucrat observes. A government that was ostensibly trying to find ways to cut back government spending, and completely reimagine how policy would be delivered, was robbed of the very people who could best tell them how to go about this. The public servant given the task of effectively dismantling the department was rather unkindly referred to by other secretaries as "Young Warwick" – a reference to young Warwick Fairfax, who had overseen a fiasco at the old family media business when he tried to buy it out just before the 1987 stock market crash, only to reduce the empire to debt-burdened rubble. The Howard government belatedly recognised the catastrophic nature of its error and sent in Ian Watt – who would later head the Department of Prime Minister and Cabinet – to try to rebuild Finance. "But you can't just put people back in the room. The memory was shot. Twenty years later, we still don't have a Department of Finance with the policy capabilities it had in 1996," a departmental source says.

What happened at Finance was the first real sign that contracting out had crossed the line and was affecting "core functions." The question in this new era was: what are the core functions of the public service? In the past it had designed and advised on policies, then delivered them. For example, it had devised ways to help the unemployed get work, then implemented them through the Commonwealth Employment Service. Treasury would be given a brief to develop a package of tax-reform measures. Now it might find itself consulted at various stages about a tax package, but not involved all along the way. The rise of the adviser was increasingly seeing policy being made "up on the hill" at Parliament House. Government departments found themselves responding to requests to provide support material for policy formulated without their input. A new term – "issues management" (meaning a department's capacity to help its minister kill off an unfavourable news story by 10 a.m.) – appeared on the scene, and was given great emphasis by many ministers. The public service was increasingly not delivering policies, but simply overseeing the contracts of those private-sector or non-government organisations that did.

The gradual change eventually hit the departments' capacity to provide advice, starting in the line departments. Specialist policy or research units suddenly found themselves both figuratively, and later literally, redundant. In the "olden days," even back in the 1980s, there was as much frisson in Canberra about the brawls between departments on a policy under development as there are now about a split in the cabinet. What happened at interdepartmental committee meetings – which powerful mandarin had done over another – was the stuff of legend. There were spectacular battles – even if they were conducted in the stilted language of the bureaucracy – that raged through the coordination comments of departments on cabinet submissions. But the crucial point is that there were, in fact, battles. Ideas were being debated and discussed at length by people with a memory of what had gone before. And, of course, they were being discussed outside the immediacy of politics. A senior public servant notes how the mission statements of departments changed during the 1990s, so that rather than saying something about maximising a particular outcome for the community, they emphasised the implementing of government policy. Ten years earlier, he says, the implicit meaning of the mission statement was that the department's job was to come up with policies framed around the "national good," not just the government's. Echoing Martin Parkinson, another senior bureaucrat notes that at some point officials in Treasury and PM&C found themselves looking around and finding that, "We didn't have anyone to talk to in other agencies." There were not people in other departments with the capacity, or the brief, or the memory, to be able to debate, or contribute to making, policy. With memory goes what is often the most powerful weapon in a bureaucrat's armoury when trying to influence a minister – or the cabinet – on a policy issue: the power of the anecdote; the power of a first-person recollection of what happened the last time something was tried. "Decades of experience is much more powerful than any considered reasoning in that sort of discussion," one official observes.

Among the central agencies, Treasury – because of the power it had gained under a series of influential treasurers – and PM&C remained immune for a lot longer. Defence, the national security establishment and Foreign Affairs were buttressed by the fact that they represent areas of policy that really are the preserve of the state.

Treasury's central role in the budget, taxation and economic forecasting allowed it to retain its stature as a policy-making body through all the economic and political travails of the last thirty years. This was despite the blow to its prestige when the recession of the early 1990s hit. But Treasury's actions in the wake of the recession – when it made a concerted effort to come to terms with, and document, the policy errors and consider what should be done in the future – show how the public service has subsequently changed, and just what gets lost in the change. In the late 1990s, the department did an extensive post-mortem on what went wrong and developed a "war-book" for how it should respond if confronted by similar circumstances in the future. The department started a process in which older officials discussed previous episodes with younger ones. Different economic scenarios were war-gamed. This was important, for even by the middle of the first decade of the century, few people were left in Treasury who had experienced the 1990s recession. What's more, as one official notes, a "belief in government intervention had been largely put beyond the memory of the current generation of politicians." In other words, Treasury went about ensuring that there was a well-documented institutional memory of what had happened for those who came afterwards.

It was Treasury's post-recession preparations that set the scene for the response to the global financial crisis in 2008. Armed with its memories of the causes of the 1990s recession and what had worked – and not worked – in getting out of it, Treasury warned the Rudd government in 2009 that big infrastructure spending and complicated projects had not worked in the early 1990s. They were too slow, and too complex and uncertain in their impact. It counselled cabinet to stick with cash payments to keep confidence up and activity ticking over. But best-laid plans can still go astray. Kevin Rudd embraced Treasury's advice on the need for a cash stimulus. But he had also become enamoured of the idea of a "double dividend" on policy, which he had picked up from Barack Obama: the idea that you could get two bangs for your buck. He looked for policies that would not only stimulate the economy but also achieve environmental outcomes. The lessons of the 1990s, documented by Treasury and delivered to the government in 2009, were not fully heeded. "He didn't want to hear it," one official says. "Double dividends were the flavour of the month." The "pink batts" scheme was born. In the tumultuous days of the GFC, there may have been people sitting around the cabinet table asking questions like, "Do we have enough home-insulation installers?" But no cabinet ministers had the authority of personal war stories with which to counter Rudd's enthusiasm for the double dividend.

It is telling that the tsunami of criticism of the Rudd government's fiscal stimulus arose from the way services and spending were delivered, and the lack of experience of the federal public service to oversee this. Years of contracting out service delivery meant there was simply no memory or experience of doing major capital works at the federal level, or of how to run a consumer-level scheme like the pink batts program. Canberra was also reliant on the states to implement the school-halls building scheme.

It wasn't as if governments weren't being warned about the structural risks of these declining capabilities. In 2009 Gary Banks, the former head of the Productivity Commission, famously warned the Rudd government that the bureaucracy no longer had the expertise to provide the "evidence-based policy" advice the prime minister was demanding. He lamented the decline in the number of public servants with the necessary quantitative and analytical skills, and warned about the varied quality and motives of the consultants involved in developing policy. While there were highly professional consultancies, he said, there were also consultants who cut corners, provided superficial reports and second-guessed what ministers wanted to hear. The contracts tended to go to business consultants rather than academics.

The problems that arose in the response to the global financial crisis were a reflection of the modern mix of public and private delivery systems, of the contracting ethos. The same was in part true of the National Broadband Network (NBN). Part of the rationale for the NBN lay in trying to fix a previous policy mistake: the decision in the Hawke–Keating years not to separate the "wholesale" and "retail" sections of the telecommunications market. Building an entirely new wholesale telecommunications framework – taking advantage of the need to upgrade the national technology – was one way of addressing this. But the sheer scale of the project, the difficulties of managing thousands of provider contracts, saw it flounder, along with the inevitable disruptions of politics. There was an immense hostility to the NBN from the Coalition from its very beginnings, in part because it represented the re-emergence of the public service as a major service provider. The Coalition in government had spent years trying to wrangle communications out of Telstra's clutches. Ironically, this only seemed to become harder when Telstra was privatised.

In a speech in June 2015, Malcolm Turnbull reflected on the fact that both private and public megaprojects always seem to have their problems:

> The history of megaprojects is such that no matter how sophisticated the technology, or how great our advances in accounting practices, we have essentially not gotten any better at avoiding serious cost overruns. One of the leading experts in the field, Bent

Flyvbjerg, looked at 111 megaprojects conducted between 1910 and 2000 and found that cost overruns have continued in fairly consistent magnitudes throughout the period. He concluded: "No learning seems to take place in this important and highly costly sector of private and public spending". Projects dealing with public spending typically tend to perform worse. Different publicly funded projects typically compete with each other for a set pool of discretionary funds, meaning there is an incentive to overcook the benefits and undercook the costs; politicians and project managers feel the need to become "advocates" to win public support for the project; and there is a natural tendency for "empire building" without adequate cost controls.

The lessons that Turnbull felt came out of the NBN experience went first to accountability, that "the architects and managers of projects need to be accountable for the things that they can deliver on and less focussed on the things they can't." Second, "risks should be assigned to those parties best equipped to deal with them." Finally, he emphasised the need for transparency and independent oversight.

If you apply Turnbull's arguments to the public service and the work of government as a whole, you have to ask yourself whether these matters of accountability, risk, transparency and independent oversight are now even remotely arranged in the best possible way, whether from the perspective of taxpayers or that of the executive government – that is, the ministry – of the day.

Intriguingly, Turnbull's response to what has happened with the NBN has not been to argue that everything the public service does is bad. It is to argue for a careful assessment of who are the best people – or organisations – to do any particular job. And that doesn't necessarily mean the private sector.

> What we have to do in government in my view is stop panning public servants and do more to ensure that they do their job better.

And one of the ways to do that is to make sure they do the work that is their core responsibility, as opposed to outsourcing every-thing. Of course, that will show up people who aren't any good too: clearly it's a lot easier just to send out a brief to McKinsey than it is to actually do the work yourself. Most people work for the public service as much for the psychic wage as they do for the financial wage. Most of the very smart people in the APS could earn a lot more money somewhere else. One of the things we've got to do is respect the public service – respect it, expect more from it, and make sure that it has more challenging and interesting work to do.

You might think that, if only for reasons of self-interest, politicians might pause to contemplate the lessons of the fiscal stimulus: that they might see beyond the attacks that attributed the problems solely to the incompetence of their political opponents. Yet in its first two years back in government, the Coalition showed few signs that it had learnt these lessons, or that it valued memory either.

Changing political fortunes meant the Coalition ended up overseeing the implementation of the largest new public sector–driven social initiative of recent decades: the National Disability Insurance Scheme (NDIS). In time, the NDIS will be a government organisation on a par in its spending, staff and spread with Australia Post or NBN Co. Yet to the puzzlement of many of those involved – including state governments – the Coalition was so determined to get its own people on the board of the NDIS that it was prepared to overhaul the scheme's entire membership, with the potential loss of memory of all those who had been there at its beginning. Even the management consultants brought in to advise the government, Korda Mentha, said board terms should be staggered, "so that there is a rolling program of board appointments. This would ensure that fresh perspec-tives, skills and experience can be brought onto the NDIA board, whilst maintaining a degree of corporate knowledge and history of the organisation."

Similarly, in the most complex and difficult area of government policy – indigenous affairs – a lack of experience seems only to have been exacerbated by decisions taken over the past couple of decades. When Tony Abbott became prime minister in 2013, he announced that he would be a prime minister for indigenous affairs and that responsibility for this area would be moved into the Department of the Prime Minister and Cabinet. Yet PM&C had no substantial infrastructure for developing or delivering indigenous policy – one of the most difficult areas of public policy. PM&C is a department that specialises in coordinating the work of the rest of the public service, not in running a major area of spending in its own right. To start with the basics, PM&C doesn't have offices around the country, let alone in remote locations. So it immediately had to assign the delivery of indigenous services to other parts of the bureaucracy.

But there is a more fundamental problem. For much of the past twenty years, since the demise of the Aboriginal and Torres Strait Islander Commission (ATSIC), there hasn't been a model – or even an organising principle – for the delivery of indigenous services. Overarching responsibility has been thrown around among departments, split up, then brought back together.

In 1996 John Howard launched a war on indigenous organisations, starting with ATSIC. The charge was financial mismanagement. ATSIC certainly had its problems, but Howard not only brought down ATSIC but also systematically broke the institutional structures of black Australia by cutting funding to bodies such as the land councils and health and legal services. Since then there have been the "interventions" and the embrace of the policies pursued on Cape York by Noel Pearson. But the approach and delivery has become erratic and utterly non-transparent. Writing in the Monthly in May 2015, Pearson described a new "Aboriginal Industry" that has grown up in place of ATSIC, which he said "is largely not comprised of blackfellas, but a vast parasitic industry of government and private-sector players":

> Consultants and service providers, ranging from Work for the Dole
> programs and employment programs, to child welfare protection

organisations, have now colonised the entire indigenous landscape … The burgeoning of this industry has largely taken place under the radar, and without critique. Because the majority of this industry is not indigenous, there is no controversy. There are no allegations of misuse and waste of money. There are no lurid media stories about misappropriate of funds.

Yet, for example, "when child protection organisations offer safe houses and foster-care homes for children, they can charge up to $5000 a week per child."

All of this remains largely invisible to us as voters and taxpayers. It is not just a matter of money, or of scandal rendered invisible. The lessons being learnt every day about the way policy works – if in fact they are being learnt – are also not being captured for future reference through the direct experience and involvement of the public service.

In total, we are talking about a massive amount of money – and policy. Pearson notes that while the Productivity Commission estimates Australia spent $30 billion on behalf of indigenous Australians in 2012–13, "indigenous-specific" funding is just $5.6 billion. The changes in the public sector mean we are spending $30 billion on a bureaucracy that is not only largely invisible to the public, but where there are no grounds for confidence that what might be learnt along the way is being documented and passed on.

Similarly, there are the mega-spending departments like Health, which itself directly administers around $40 billion of government spending. These run on more traditional public service lines and have more transparency to their operations. But it is not clear that they necessarily have any greater focus on, or memory of, policy. In 2011 the Australian Public Service Commission began systematic reviews of government agencies to assess how effective they were.

The review of the Department of Health, released in December 2014, has become a minor classic of the genre. It is written in the strangled modern language of the public service – an excruciating blend of bureaucratese and managerialism – but even so, a disturbing picture emerges. The review team regularly heard examples of risk aversion, tight control of information and micro-management, coupled with the reluctance of a number of employees to report potential risks or mistakes due to fear of being blamed for failures. This had created "blind spots" to risk. The report noted an "excessive focus on issues management" and said:

> internal and external interviewees commented on the department's centralised and elevated approach to decision making, which they identified was the product of a command-and-control leadership style and a risk-averse culture. While this approach may be useful for emergency or crisis management, employees and a number of external stakeholders observed it has disempowered the SES [the department's senior management], created vertical work silos, limited ownership of direction setting and decision making, and stifled innovation.
>
> Regular weekly meetings convened with the Secretary, deputy secretaries and first assistant secretaries ... largely focus on managing issues, reputational risk and matters related to corporate services and systems. There was little evidence in Executive Leadership Team meeting agendas provided to the review of high-level discussions on organisational strategy or policy.

A picture emerges of a department that is so busy sorting out its own issues, and dousing fires for ministers, that it has little time to think about ways to improve the health of the nation. In all that long critique, you may have noticed that the word "policy" appears just once.

Whatever the shortcomings of the health department at the time of the review, it has changed further since then, in ways which make you wonder once more about the institutional memory of those running the department. The then secretary of the department, Jane Halton, was promoted to the Department of Finance at the end of 2014. Around the same time, the government announced it was merging the immigration and

Never again miss an issue. Subscribe and save.

☐ **1 year print and digital subscription** (4 issues) $79.95 (incl. GST).
Subscriptions outside Australia $119.95.

☐ **2 year print and digital subscription** (8 issues) $129.95 (incl. GST).

☐ **1 year digital only subscription** $39.95 (incl. GST)

☐ Tick here to commence subscription with the current issue.
All prices include postage and handling.

PAYMENT DETAILS I enclose a cheque/money order made out to Schwartz Publishing Pty Ltd.
Or please debit my credit card (MasterCard, Visa or Amex accepted).

CARD NO.

EXPIRY DATE   /   CCV   AMOUNT $

CARDHOLDER'S NAME

SIGNATURE

NAME

ADDRESS

EMAIL   PHONE

tel: (03) 9486 0288 **fax:** (03) 9486 0244 **email:** subscribe@blackincbooks.com **www.quarterlyessay.com**

An inspired gift. Subscribe a friend.

☐ **1 year print and digital subscription** (4 issues) $79.95 (incl. GST).
Subscriptions outside Australia $119.95.

☐ **2 year print and digital subscription** (8 issues) $129.95 (incl. GST).

☐ **1 year digital only subscription** $39.95 (incl. GST)

☐ Tick here to commence subscription with the current issue.
All prices include postage and handling.

PAYMENT DETAILS I enclose a cheque/money order made out to Schwartz Publishing Pty Ltd.
Or please debit my credit card (MasterCard, Visa or Amex accepted).

CARD NO.

EXPIRY DATE   /   CCV   AMOUNT $

CARDHOLDER'S NAME   SIGNATURE

NAME

ADDRESS

EMAIL   PHONE

RECIPIENT'S NAME

RECIPIENT'S ADDRESS

tel: (03) 9486 0288 **fax:** (03) 9486 0244 **email:** subscribe@blackincbooks.com **www.quarterlyessay.com**

Delivery Address:
LEVEL 1, 221 DRUMMOND ST
CARLTON VIC 3053

Quarterly Essay
REPLY PAID 90094
CARLTON VIC 3053

Delivery Address:
LEVEL 1, 221 DRUMMOND ST
CARLTON VIC 3053

Quarterly Essay
REPLY PAID 90094
CARLTON VIC 3053

customs departments into the militaristically minded Border Force. Many of the people working in Immigration were underwhelmed by the change and voted with their feet. Many followed their former department head, Martin Bowles, to the health department. The Canberra Times reported in July 2015 that Immigration "now faces the public service's greatest executive brain drain since the 1980s with a quarter of its upper ranks either shown the door or turning their back on the department since its takeover by Customs."

> The Canberra Times has confirmed the toll of departures, either already announced or coming up, has reached 30, from a senior executive cohort of 119 in June 2014. Four deputy secretaries, nine first assistant secretaries and 17 assistant secretaries have now confirmed their departures or are expected soon to do so. An unprecedented 10 of them have opted to follow their old boss Martin Bowles to the Health Department. Insiders have complained about the management style of the new regime and there has been unhappiness from veteran public servants forced to wear the military-style Australian Border Force uniform to work each day after a lifetime of civilian service. Many of the replacement executives drafted in have come from Defence, where new Immigration secretary Michael Pezzullo used to work.

So Health is now being run by Immigration experts. Border Force is peopled by bureaucrats from Defence.

*

In 1985 a young Ken Henry peered around the corner of a cubicle he occupied in the basement of the Treasury building, where the officials working on Paul Keating's tax reform options were housed. "What are you working on?" he asked the man at the next desk. "I'm designing a capital gains tax!" an equally youthful Martin Parkinson responded enthusiastically.

Tax policy is one of the best ways of telling the story of changes in public policy-making in the last thirty years. It remains an area of great contention and public interest. It is one of the few remaining areas of economic decision-making that has not been lost to government by deregulation – as has, say, wages policy or interest-rate regulation. It was an area where, as a joint project with the government of the day, the public service – Treasury – had a massive influence throughout the 1980s and 1990s. Tax reform saw the introduction of a comprehensive (if mild) capital gains tax, the fringe benefits tax, dividend imputation, a drawn-out debate about federal wholesale taxes and their replacement by a federal consumption tax (or GST) and the elimination of less efficient taxes. It saw a range of new ideas, such as international competitiveness, building national saving and new tax bases that made the most of changing technologies. Tax policy was also transformed by technology shifting the way money moved around the globe. Between the 1980s and 2015, the debate gradually got bogged down in brawls over smaller changes to the tax mix, rather than the brave new world of new taxes and major tax shifts contemplated by Parkinson and Henry in the Treasury basement. There was, inevitably, a massive expansion in the size of tax legislation, rulings and case law. This created its own problems for the bureaucrats.

Martin Parkinson was there at the beginning of the tax reform discussion. He remembers all the brawls and policy modifications along the way. But thirty years later, Treasury has a lot of trouble recruiting people into its tax division. Recruits contemplate their prospects if they go into tax policy: the sheer complexity means several years' investment in getting up to speed before you can give any decent advice – if, that is, the government of the day is prepared to listen.

In the dying days of the Gillard government, Treasury was hit by the harsh redundancies imposed across the public service by a government desperate to meet its pledge to return the budget to surplus. Staffing levels were slashed. Among the voluntary redundancies, it tended to be the older staff who left. Most of them were in tax – known as the revenue group. Many of the older and more senior staff in this area were the last of those who had come through the ranks during the era of big change under Paul Keating and Peter Costello. A total of sixty-two staff took redundancies or were made redundant over the three years from 2012 to 2014. Even as Treasury was being asked to prepare for a new round of tax reform – in conjunction with a group in Treasurer Joe Hockey's office – its tax division had a third less staff than it had three years earlier.

This is just one example of serious, continuing, real-world implications for the way Australia is governed, flowing from what has happened to the public service in the past thirty years. It is not just about politicisation. It is a result of politicians failing to value and preserve our institutions.

Numbers, as always, can tell a story. My *Australian Financial Review* colleague Verona Burgess has pointed out that, according to the Australian Public Service Commission, the median length of service of "ongoing" public servants in mid-2014 was 9.4 years. "So only about half the core workforce had a working life in the [public service] extending back as far as the last couple of years of the Howard government." Similarly, almost 40 per cent of public servants are aged below forty, so that "the 1975 dismissal is beyond ancient history, the Fraser government barely, if at all, a memory and the Hawke government probably background noise to their childhood." In other words, about half the public service doesn't remember the place working any differently to the way it has worked from the Howard era onwards – cannot recall a time when policy-makers in departments had a real role to play and there was a vital and active engagement with executive government. The problem isn't the youth of the public service now. The Seven Dwarfs at the height of their influence were young and dynamic and full of new ideas. It is the lack of mechanisms by which talented up-and-coming recruits can gain access to the experience of their elders: it is that the public service, despite losing much memory through change and falling numbers, doesn't have the processes in place to keep those institutional memories alive. Ultimately, it is as though we as a community have ceased to recognise what a valuable repository of memory, and what a valuable institution, the public service is.

THE DECAY OF WESTMINSTER

Malcolm Turnbull strode into the Senate Courtyard of Parliament House in Canberra at 4 p.m. on 14 September 2015 and announced he had challenged Tony Abbott for the Liberal Party leadership and, therefore, the prime ministership. "It is clear enough that the Government is not successful in providing the economic leadership that we need," he said. "It is not the fault of individual ministers. Ultimately the Prime Minister has not been capable of providing the economic leadership our nation needs; he has not been capable of providing the economic confidence that business needs."

Turnbull's move was immediately portrayed by the media in the language of the coup against Kevin Rudd. Yet unlike in 2010, a challenge to Tony Abbott's leadership had been a clear prospect for months, as the government languished in the polls and went from political disaster to political disaster. Turnbull had emerged as the only real alternative candidate. The sole surprise was in the timing of the challenge: before the Canning by-election, not after it. Abbott had, after all, been mortally wounded in a political sense in February, and been unable to recover the government's fortunes. Unlike in 2010, the Turnbull challenge came about because Abbott's most senior front-bench colleagues moved against him, having concluded that the government simply could not continue. It was not a political assassination by a bunch of nonentities recently arrived in parliament and more accustomed to playing factional politics in the Labor movement. The only true similarity was in the bringing down of a first-term prime minister. None of this stopped Tony Abbott and his supporters from trying in every way they could to paint the change to Turnbull as a re-run of 2010. They used the same language about assassins in the night and, rather overlooking the realities of our electoral system, argued that it was for voters, not MPs, to elect a prime minister.

This dressing up of the Turnbull challenge as the Gillard coup was an attempt to de-legitimise it; to load all the sorry history of the Labor years onto current events in the minds of both the waverers in Coalition ranks and the electorate.

Whatever the mechanics of the drama, yet one more thing that was utterly different was that Turnbull, unlike Julia Gillard, was able to say why he was challenging. It wasn't just about the polls, no matter how much they helped to focus the minds of his colleagues. It was about the way government and politics were working. It was an exciting time to be alive, Turnbull told voters, in clear contrast to the fearful messages of Abbott. The country faced challenges and opportunities:

> We need a style of leadership that explains those challenges and opportunities; explains the challenges and how to seize the opportunities. A style of leadership that respects the peoples' intelligence, that explains these complex issues, and then sets out the course of action we believe we should take, and makes a case for it. We need advocacy, not slogans. We need to respect the intelligence of the Australian people ...
>
> We also need a new style of leadership in the way we deal with others, whether it is our fellow Members of Parliament, whether it is the Australian people. We need to restore traditional Cabinet Government. There must be an end to policy on the run and captain's calls. We need to be truly consultative with colleagues, Members of Parliament, Senators and the wider public. We need an open Government ... that recognises that there is an enormous sum of wisdom both within our colleagues in this building and of course further afield.

To outsiders, talk of new styles of leadership and the restoration of cabinet government didn't mean much. International coverage of the change marvelled at how Australia had managed to have five prime ministers in five years. The *Economist* was typical when it asked whether Australia's economy could be "fixed by a system that produces so many political assassinations." Malcolm Turnbull's ascension has restarted the clock on the question of whether there is something inherently wrong with the way politics works in Australia, or whether we have merely seen a freak series of events.

The fall of Abbott, and the return of Turnbull, provoked much discussion of the role of prime minister's offices. Equally, there was plenty of speculation about whether Turnbull would repeat his mistakes as Opposition leader in the way he dealt with people. But there has not been quite so much about the more fundamental question of whether the revolving door of the prime ministership has much deeper causes than the personalities in Parliament House. Is the question whether Malcolm Turnbull – and those around him – can learn from history? Or is there a structural reason national politics has become so dysfunctional?

*

There is a quote from the American gonzo journalist Hunter S. Thompson stuck up on a piece of yellowing paper above my desk in the Parliament House press gallery:

> Most nights are slow in the politics business, but every once and a while you get a fast one, a blast of wild treachery and weirdness that not even the hard boys can handle.

I first came across the quote in the Hawke era. It encapsulated a particularly wild ride during the months in 1991 when Paul Keating resigned as treasurer and stalked Bob Hawke, apparently prepared to bring down the government in the quest to replace him as leader.

There have been plenty of occasions on which to recall Thompson's words since then, of course. It feels as though the fast and wild nights in politics have become more frequent. Yet there had been almost a decade of leadership coups and counter-coups in the Liberal Party by the time Labor's leadership drama came to a head in 1991. Granted, these were about the Opposition leadership, not the leadership of the government. That was what made the Hawke–Keating tussle – along with the sheer size of the personalities of the two men – so extraordinary when it finally came to a head.

Seen from today's perspective, though, the notable thing about the wild nights on both sides of politics until 2010 was that they would quickly settle down again into some form of normality and sense of order. Of course there were wounds to be licked and resentments that would never quite go away. But government – and even Opposition – would quickly refocus on the task at hand. The wild nights were a bizarre aberration. It was almost as if the blast of treachery had all been part of the plan for orderly government, rather than something that fundamentally threatened it. And in general, we, the voters, were not worse off as a result of that wild treachery.

The first real sign that those fast nights in politics were now in the hands of amateurs came in June 2010, when the Labor Caucus overthrew a first-term prime minister. Here was a coup that was ill-conceived, ill-constructed and catastrophic, one that showed us how such manoeuvring could have a material impact on the rest of us. For normal government didn't resume the next day.

The shock to the system that night wasn't just in the way it erupted, seemingly from nowhere. It was in what it told us – what it confirmed – about how the Labor Party had changed since Keating stalked Hawke in 1991. That earlier battle had been about an ageing government. It was between two figures broadly seen as joint authors of that government's political and policy success. The case was for renewal and new ideas. There was no real suggestion in 2010 that policy principle might be at stake, or even policy or political competence. Julia Gillard told us that the government had lost its way. A Labor frontbencher famously summed up the depth of thought that went into it when he said to the ABC's Chris Uhlmann on the afternoon of the coup, "So, do you think we can win with Julia?" Much later, she and many of her colleagues said it was because Kevin Rudd was out of control. It was about personal hatred and about the polls.

David Marr writes in his Quarterly Essay on Bill Shorten, *Faction Man*, about Labor's powerful Victorian Right faction, and in doing so paints a picture of what has happened to the Labor Party in recent decades:

> They do politics differently there. Wars are fought in the name of peace. Explosives are packed under the foundations of the Labor Party in the name of stability. They call the wreckage left after these brawls rejuvenation. The wonder is that Victoria delivers any Labor talent to Canberra and remains, decade after decade, a stronghold of the party.

Marr says the factions ceased fighting over policy decades ago. "All that was at stake in the conflicts that had shaken the party for over a decade were places in parliament. In no other party and no other state has so much political blood been split for half a metre of leather."

The Victorian Right was at the heart of the 2010 coup. It had brought the factional manouverings to Canberra in an unprecedented way: you executed the person in the same way as usual. It didn't seem to occur to anyone that the fact he was prime minister made this different to an internal brawl.

Our perception of collective order and faith in "the system" was deeply undermined on that night in 2010, both by the coup itself, but more importantly by the failure to re-establish some sense of control and strategy in its wake. Many people believed that this was simply due to a Labor Party that had become deeply corrupted, leached of any real talent, and which was, as a result, imploding. But there were more shocks to come. Many believed that the confronting sense of loss of political order could be dealt with by changing the government, getting rid of the dysfunctional Labor Party and putting Tony Abbott and the Coalition into office. Voters were prepared to believe Tony Abbott when he said that he would bring back "adult government"; that he could call a halt to the chaos. Yet eighteen months later, the first and predominant words voters used in focus groups to describe the prime minister were "idiot" and "fool."

Instead of a government that went about its business delivering sensible, articulated policy, voters got broken promises of a spectacular magnitude and a politics of three-word slogans which seemed perpetually stuck in the mode of opposition. Everything the government had to say, it seemed, was about the Labor Party.

This was a profound moment for Australian politics. It now seemed that all the uncertainty of the preceding years might not be due solely to the manoeuvrings of Labor's faceless men – instead, both sides of politics were unable to run the country!

The tendency to ascribe all fault to individual personality or management style is understandable when leadership struggles are such human dramas. But it does not explain why a succession of prime ministers have succumbed to the preconditions – the series of political misjudgments that cause colleagues to lose faith in their leader – which ultimately led to their downfall. A run of bad opinion polls, or some final political debacle, might trigger the actual leadership challenge, but these things don't explain what made those prime ministers so vulnerable in the first place.

Australians have long been rude about their politicians. But there has been an underlying faith in the governance of the place. Kevin Rudd enjoyed stratospheric popularity with the public, even if his colleagues loathed him, until just a couple of months before his fall in 2010. Julia Gillard struggled with minority government and internal dissension throughout her prime ministership. Tony Abbott had clearer air than either of them: a smashed Labor Party, a voting public that had been warned it would have to cop tough medicine and was desperate for stability, and complete internal party discipline through his first twelve months, even if voters were at best ambivalent about him.

Commentators have mused on whether voters have come to see politics as a reality television show and have the same tolerance – and appetite – for the weakest performer to be rapidly "voted off." This might explain, the argument goes, voters' rush to judgment on prime ministers of late.

But the attitude of voters doesn't explain what has happened here: remember it was the political players in the Rudd coup who thought they were going to gain the approval of the mob for their actions, and it was the mob that reacted with horror.

The only constancies across these three prime ministerships are the stories of dysfunction within the cabinet and government, of too much unchallenged prime ministerial power, and of disastrous political judgments. So the bigger question is why politicians on both sides have not been able to govern competently but instead have compulsively repeated the political and policy mistakes of their predecessors. At the very least, it suggests the political and administrative mechanisms aren't in place to save prime ministers from themselves and their brilliant, middle-of-the-night ideas.

The fall of Tony Abbott provoked a renewed focus on prime ministerial offices and government processes, particularly around his controversial chief of staff, Peta Credlin. Those with longer memories note two particular features of the offices of Kevin Rudd, Julia Gillard and Tony Abbott. Most notably, none of them opted for chiefs of staff with long bureaucratic experience. The point is not that public servants are the fount of all wisdom: it is that they know how the public service works and what it can, and can't, do for you. Having a public servant running your office also implies a degree of respect for the institution of the public service, rather than the hostility that Tony Abbott and his office exuded, or even the unreasonable expectations put on it by Kevin Rudd; it suggests that you understand government is something a lot larger than politicians alone. The most successful periods of the most successful, and lengthy, prime ministerships of recent times – those of Bob Hawke and John Howard – saw the prime minister's office run by people with public service backgrounds, or on secondment from the public service.

The second noteworthy thing about the offices of successful and unsuccessful recent prime ministers is that the successful ones clearly delineated the roles of a chief of staff who ran the government and a political adviser who contemplated the politics. With these two streams of advice distinguished, prime ministers could consider both the political and policy aspects of any decision. This also allowed a further distinction: between past and present. Both the political present and a policy framework that had continuity with all that had gone before could be clearly considered on their own merits.

In Abbott's case, adopting such an approach may have also helped break up the "institutional" structures that had been so successful in Opposition, but which proved disastrous in government. As Opposition leader, Abbott worked with an immensely tight, immensely successful, immensely small group of staffers and political colleagues. Opposition leaders are given vast latitude by their colleagues to make "captain's calls" on policy in the interests of political expediency.

Abbott was one of our longest-serving Opposition leaders in recent times. Breaking out of the habits of several years of working with just this group and seeing the need to transform modus operandi when it came to running a cabinet government was always going to be difficult. The mistrust of outsiders in the Abbott office, however, meant that, if anything, even more people were frozen out once the Coalition won government.

In 2014 Rod Rhodes and Anne Tiernan published *The Gatekeepers: Lessons from Prime Ministers' Chiefs of Staff*, which documents conversations with prime ministerial chiefs of staff going back to the Fraser years. The book notes that bureaucratic secondments to ministerial offices had dropped sharply from the days of Hawke and Keating, when up to 70 per cent of staffers were seconded from the public service. The growing tendency for politicians to target or label public servants politically means time in a ministerial office – once seen as an invaluable experience for public servants – is now seen as a career negative. The benefit of the old crossover between public service and ministerial offices, Rhodes and Tiernan argue, was that "public servants understood the pressures and contingencies of ministerial life. Ministers understood how the public service could help them." They conclude: "Both politicians and public servants [now have] less knowledge of how government works and the amount and quality of expert advice was reduced."

This lack of institutional memory affects everything about the way our politics plays out. For a start, bureaucrats who stay on while the political players change might recognise old ideas. Former Labor ministers were genuinely surprised after the 2014 budget that the new government had simply picked up the same raw policy proposals the public service had been serving up for years and included them in the budget. Their argument was that these were not things rejected by Labor on ideological grounds, or because they were too hard politically, but because they required significant work to turn them from public policy goals into part of a coherent budget strategy, part of a political sales job, one which had some chance of getting through the Senate. This highlights how successful outcomes have tended to be a joint production of good policy-makers and savvy politicians who know how to shape a policy into something they can sell. Their conclusion was that, whatever else you said about such policies, it seemed no one in the new government (which ended up racing to put its budget together) recognised these as coming from the bureaucracy's bottom drawer. Similarly, a Coalition MP remarked to a Labor MP when Labor was in government that he couldn't believe Labor had been dumb enough to take up public service proposals to change employee share-ownership schemes that the Howard government had rejected as politically unworkable. These changes went on to cause all sorts of problems not just for the Rudd and Gillard governments but also for entrepreneurs seeking to finance their start-up companies.

In fact, the lack of policy memory in ministers' office has on occasion led them to rely too much on the bureaucracy. A case in point was the incoming Rudd government. It commissioned the Henry Review to produce a "cutting-edge" paper on tax reform, not just for the next election but looking ahead to the next couple of decades. And that's what it got. Measures like the mining super-profits tax were still at a theoretical stage. No one involved in their development anticipated that they would be adopted as they were. The experience of Ken Henry and others in the Treasury over twenty years had been to have their ideas mashed up, stomped on and reworked into something political.

Michael Thawley, now the head of PM&C, was one very senior bureaucrat who did move from the public service into a prime ministerial office, when he became John Howard's international adviser in 1996. At the 2015 conference of the ACT division of the Institute of Public Administration Australia, he told his audience that the best way they could contribute was to bring their expertise and their view from outside into the sanctums of executive government.

> John Howard used to say to me when I first arrived in his office and I was trying to be politically sensitive, "I'd like to know what you think about international relations. Leave the politics to me. I'll work out how to do it." And I think that is the way we need to think.

Thawley identifies the simple but often overlooked truth that politicians think differently to policy experts. Another senior public servant who worked in ministerial offices observes: "Politicians are politicians. That is what they do. We shouldn't be surprised or shocked by that. They are always looking at an issue from a political perspective. Our job is to make sure that they can see ways that marry the politics with the policy imperatives."

Don Russell returned to Canberra during the Gillard period as secretary of the industry department, and in 2014 he reflected on the day-to-day realities of relationships among prime ministers, ministers, advisers and the public service. Watching from the outside, he said, we tend to presume that prime minister's offices know what the rest of the government is doing. And since Australia is supposed to be run by cabinet governments, we also assume there is an agreed policy work plan. But, as Russell noted, "It can be exceedingly nerve-racking for a Prime Minister and his or her staff to know that they are surrounded in the Executive Wing of

Parliament House by a group of Ministers who are working away on bright ideas guided only by the enthusiasms of their staff."

In other words, not all prime ministers want their ministers guided by political staffers alone. Russell's message to the public service was to become less risk-averse and change a modus operandi which only responds to ministerial requests. Public service departments had to understand (and perhaps learn again) that advice was contestable. They should anticipate where policy discussions would go, all the better to be able to assert what ministers needed to know, and therefore be included in the discussions. Thawley had the same message:

> Most of us joined the public service not because we wanted a job forever but because we had ideas about how Australia should be, what sort of a place we wanted our country to be, what sort of society we wanted. That's what the government needs and that's what it wants to hear. It doesn't want a supine public service. It wants to know what we think, what ideas we have for making changes and how to make them happen.

Some parties will disagree, of course. According to one former adviser, even as the influence – and memories – of seasoned bureaucrats has been fading from ministerial offices, there has been a maturation of a generation of political staffers at a time when the "dark arts" of spin and politics have been professionalised to a much greater extent. Research – as in political research – he argues, has given staffers a false sense of confidence that you "can do it by numbers" – that you can find your way through to a policy option purely by political judgment, by focus-group testing different ideas and avoiding any dangerous ones. But that also means policy is viewed purely in its current context. The history of any particular political and policy issue is *so* yesterday.

The dominance of the dark arts and catchy slogans in achieving success in Opposition puts policy development and the prospects for cabinet consultation on the back foot too, even before a new government is sworn in.

In a "disciplined" and successful Opposition – and this was true of both Labor under Rudd, and the Coalition under Abbott – power is inevitably ceded to the leader's office. The cost, when finally you get into government, is that the only experience of power relationships on the front bench is of an almost presidential supremacy. Ministers sometimes come to office too cowed to make an executive decision.

That has helped kill off memories of another aspect of successful cabinet governments: the prime minister as chair of the board. Bob Hawke was famous for his chairmanship of cabinet – for giving all of his ministers both a voice and a sense of ownership over the government's collective decisions. John Howard also managed his cabinet successfully. In more recent years, particularly under Kevin Rudd and Tony Abbott, it has felt more as though ministers were an annoyance to be dealt with.

This is the backdrop against which Malcolm Turnbull argues he will restore true cabinet government: that is, a government where the policy issues of the day are decided by the full cabinet after discussion of proposals put forward by individual ministers.

*

The presidential focus on the leaders has not only left ministers out of the general gaze – unless they stuff up – it has also rendered backbench MPs and senators virtually invisible and with much less scope to develop their parliamentary, political and policy skills.

When I ask politicians, and those who congregate around them, why things have become so difficult, the constant culprit named is the "24/7 media cycle." So often is it cited as the cause of all political evil that it sometimes seems to have ended thought about how political life has changed in other ways. I refuse to believe it is so simple. Politicians certainly feel that they have to feed the media beast at all times, lest someone else occupy the space. Yet the quandary is why, when the media have so many hours to fill, and when the platforms on which politicians can speak have multiplied to such a degree, they still argue that it is impossible to get their message out.

A real problem is that the passage of time and the relatively short professional life of most politicians mean most cannot remember a time when it was different. It was once the case that ministers doing an interview spoke only on their own portfolio. If journalists asked them about other issues, they would politely demur and say that this wasn't in their area of portfolio responsibility so it would not be appropriate to comment, or that they weren't well-enough informed to be able to comment. I sometimes mention this to staffers and politicians, who invariably don't know it and cannot fathom that you would pass up an opportunity to pronounce on something, even if you have no idea what you are talking about. A calm and confident refusal – on the grounds of ignorance – is seen as politically risky. The need to comment has attained ludicrous levels of inanity. Each day, the leader's office (on both sides of politics) circulates "talking points" full of glib phrases, about any issue or controversy that might arise, in the hope that it will stop MPs going "off-message." All it produces is politicians spouting a lot of glib phrases. If politicians are going to go "off-message," they still will, by conscious choice or spectacular accident.

Politicians are not just given talking points to break out if they venture to speak to the media. One long-serving member notes with derision that his leader's office sends out points for use in the weekly period when MPs make short ninety-second statements in the parliament about electoral matters. The only challenge here is how you, for example, get "We have stopped the boats" into a contribution noting the success of one of your local netball teams in the regional comp.

Press releases are now often generated centrally. "It used to be the case that, as an Opposition frontbencher – or even as a backbencher – if you wanted to put out a press release, you'd do all your own research about the issue, write it up, and then you would send it out," this MP tells me. "Not anymore!"

In the House of Representatives, there is now little incentive to put much effort into parliamentary debates. That's not because the government controls the numbers – it always has – but because nobody listens to parliament anymore. The public doesn't listen and, for that matter, neither do the politicians, who are usually sitting back in their offices getting on with other business. A speech in the House was once an occasion for MPs to make a mark.

People often lament the declining diversity in the life experience of new parliamentarians and argue that this is a reason for the drabness of politics. I would argue a counter-case. Whatever the background of the politicians coming into parliament, the decline of chamber debate as a platform for ambitious politicians means many members of the House of Representatives never have to learn to be parliamentarians. That is, they don't have to learn about, engage in and be able to advocate or explain the context of policy decisions, let alone the decisions themselves. They don't have to learn parliamentary negotiation. Some of them, as a result, don't understand that parliament is about negotiation. The fact that Tony Abbott never bothered to meet the crossbench senators who held the key to much of his legislation reflects an unfortunately common ignorance and contempt for the Senate and its processes in the lower house. It was a point of pride for Kevin Rudd and much of his cabinet that they would not negotiate with, or even talk to, the Greens.

The capacity of politicians to absorb the institutional memory of the parliament itself has therefore been degraded. A House of Reps backbencher's only detailed exposure to a policy issue, and the government's legislative response, might be if they happen to sit on a parliamentary committee examining that issue, or that legislation.

It is really only in the crossbench senators that we still see the dramatic impact that a parliamentary life can have on individuals and their views. Crossbench senators are forced to become experts in more or less everything that goes through the parliament. They are lobbied on everything, forced to debate everything, down to clause-by-clause detail on contentious legislation. People with limited life, political or policy experience suddenly blossom under the onslaught of exposure to complex issues. Think of how the much-ridiculed Jacqui Lambie, Ricky Muir,

Glenn Lazarus and Dio Wang have developed since they entered parliament in July 2014. They are the best examples of what happens when people are exposed to the institutional memory of not just the bureaucracy and the parliament, but of all the lobbyists and others with an interest in an issue.

The rise and rise of presidential-style politics has infected every aspect of the way politicians' days are shaped. In Question Time, almost all the questions go to the prime minister, rather than his or her ministers. The driving force is getting the "grab" for the evening news. The days when an Opposition would ask questions of other ministers, or even "pick off" the weakest minister in a government, seem long past. Even more forgotten are times when oppositions asked questions seeking information, and government ministers took seriously the task of answering them.

*

History and memory are astonishingly potent weapons in politics. This is particularly important at a time when the major political parties are institutions that, in historical terms, are a little bereft of a cause. Labor, the Liberals and the Nationals have all moved far from where they started, as the social and political institutions that helped define them have disappeared. Labor doesn't really have an ideology anymore. In fact, it spends quite a lot of its time trying not to have an ideology. The Coalition, on the other hand, found itself becoming increasingly ideological under Tony Abbott's leadership, but voters were somewhat perplexed at what they had apparently endorsed at the 2013 election. If it is not so clear anymore why, as an organisation, you exist, it only becomes more imperative to define yourself by the history of your actions.

Reflecting on Tony Abbott's fall in September, the *Economist* noted that:

> The old class-bound lines, along which Liberal and Labor loyalties once ran, have gone. Both parties are now hunting on the same ground, among an urban, educated swing-voting middle class.

When confronted by the findings of the latest opinion polls or focus groups, the parties' tendency is to panic; the next election is never far away.

With ideology absent or confused, the battle for the swinging voter who is unaligned in an ideological sense increases the apparent risks of standing for anything. It also increases the difficulty of defining what you stand for.

But as time goes by, the memories tend to over-glorify the past, and under-comprehend how it came about. The classic case in recent Australian history is that of the period of reform in the 1980s and 1990s. Labor likes to claim it as utterly its own: only Labor had the courage and capacity to take risky policy decisions and pursue unpopular reforms which led to the transformation of the economy. By contrast, the Coalition has argued that these changes could not have been achieved without its assistance and that it was really all its own agenda. Hazy memories of Bob Hawke's "consensus" politics tend further to blur the memory of what happened into some golden period of universal agreement about the need for change – in stark contrast to the one we face now.

Just as important in determining the history of the 1980s and 1990s were the motivations and political perceptions of the times. With the political memory of the Whitlam government still fresh, Labor was perennially on the back foot and desperate to prove its economic credentials. The Coalition was always seen as the party that the business establishment believed would undertake much harder-line reform. That meant that the Coalition's struggle through the 1980s and 1990s increasingly became one of proving to voters that it wasn't too hardline. In other words, not much has changed in the way voters see the two parties today.

The competition to "write" the history of any period becomes even more intense as a vehicle for explaining to voters, in memories that are comfortably familiar, what you stand for. One of the benefits of winning a political battle is the likelihood that your version will be the one remembered.

The myth of Howard's support for Labor's reforms still powerfully plays out in our politics. Tony Abbott and Joe Hockey and their colleagues regularly asserted that the Coalition supported Labor's economic reforms in the 1980s as a way of gaining ownership of them.

Yet blurred memories of past glories can have devastating effects. When Tony Abbott won government in 2013, it was with a promise that he would bring back the glory days of Howard. For much of his cabinet, who had been part of the declining end of the Howard years, that meant simply taking what they believed to be Howard government plays out of the book and repeating them. Nowhere was this more obvious than in the 2014 budget.

The Coalition had been quite open about its political strategy even before it won office. It would arrive without having made many positive proposals; it would spend its first term getting rid of various Labor policies against which it had campaigned; and it would fix the budget to establish a strong foundation from which to go into a second term.

The Coalition's absolute belief that it could simply replicate what John Howard and Peter Costello had done was something to behold. It refused to recognise or contemplate the many changes that had taken place since 1996. In 1996 the economy was lifting out of a savage recession. The revenue bases of the government had started to snap back into shape, as they had always done in the past. A new – and what would eventually prove historic – resources boom was around the corner. In addressing the budget, Howard and Costello had thirteen years of Labor policy to undo or reshape.

The exceptionally different circumstances that would confront Tony Abbott and Joe Hockey were hardly a secret. The world economy had been failing to extricate itself from the aftermath of the global financial crisis. Australia's revenue bases had collapsed. Our boom was over and we had already spent the proceeds well into the future by giving ourselves unsustainable tax cuts. There were only a few years of Labor policy to undo, even if there had been an explosion of government spending after the GFC.

Yet this all came as a real shock to the Coalition when it finally won office. It had believed its own story that all the problems lay with the incompetence of Labor. It had refused to countenance that some things really had changed.

History remains the most intense of political battlefields. No one understands that better than Tony Abbott, who, in the wake of his fall, set about attempting to rewrite the history of the challenge and to nobble his successor by claiming that Malcolm Turnbull was keeping to his plan. It was a Shakespearean moment: Tony Abbott, the Julius Caesar assassinated for overstepping his powers, was suddenly playing the part of Mark Antony at the Roman forum telling us that Brutus was an honourable man.

At a time when the old ideological divides have faded and been transformed, history has become an even more potent part of the political play. Ironically, though, in the way politics is actually conducted our leaders regularly take catastrophic decisions either because they have hazy memories of what has gone before, or because they work in structures that don't require them to consider history and experience. Without the ballast of memory, it is hardly surprising that they often seem to be so little in control of where they are going.

TABLOID TIMES

The Crimean War is well-nigh forgotten today, save for the Charge of the Light Brigade, Florence Nightingale and, in Australia, a legacy of streets named Balaclava and Sebastopol. As the historian Orlando Figes noted in his 2012 book, *The Crimean War: A History*, there would not be many people who could say what it was all about, even in the states that fought, which included Russia, Britain, France, Piedmont-Sardinia in Italy and the Ottoman Empire, and even though *three-quarters of a million* soldiers died in the conflict. "Historians have tended to dismiss the religious motives of the war," he writes:

> Few devote more than a paragraph or two to the dispute in the Holy Land – the rivalry between the Catholics or Latins (backed by France) and the Greeks (supported by Russia) over who should have control of the Church of the Holy Sepulchre in Jerusalem and the Church of the Nativity in Bethlehem ... Until the religious wars of our own age, it seemed implausible that a petty quarrel over some churchwarden's keys should entangle the great powers in a major war.

Instead, the war has been seen as an outcome of imperial rivalries and the actions of statesmen.

The context in which we understand the past fluctuates over time, influenced by contemporary events and changing fashions of thought. Think how Shakespeare's *Henry V* is regularly reimagined and reinterpreted every few years through the prism of contemporary fascinations. As Figes says, we might now understand the Crimean War as a religious war rather than an imperial one because religion, in the last couple of decades, has suddenly re-emerged as a recognised cause of war and a present danger to the Western world. But you could equally argue that our focus on ideological struggles of a political nature, and our ignorance of the past, incline us to see religious wars as something totally new – when of course they are not.

What is fascinating about Figes's book for my purposes, though, is that he doesn't just tell the story of the bleak battles in the freezing or roasting conditions of the Crimean peninsula, or of the machinations of the political leaders of the day, but sets events in a broader context:

> This was a war – the first war in history – to be brought about by the pressure of the press and by public opinion. With the development of the railways enabling the emergence of a national press in the 1840s and 1850s, public opinion became a potent force in British politics, arguably overshadowing the influence of Parliament and the cabinet itself.

The aggression of the press then – not just in Britain, but in all the nations involved – is truly shocking, even to our jaundiced eyes, especially in contrast to our impressions of polite Victorian England. Yet seen from the standpoint of Australia in 2015, there is also something depressingly familiar in the way an angry populace and media drove events 160 years ago, and how war was used for political purposes.

Figes argues that the British prime minister, Lord Palmerston, was the first modern politician to understand "the need to cultivate the press and appeal in simple terms to the public in order to create a mass-based political constituency." Palmerston became so popular, "and his foreign policy became so closely linked to the defence of 'British values' in the public mind, that anyone who tried to halt the drift to war was likely to be vilified by the patriotic press."

If you think the media – here and in other Western countries – can be a little feral these days, consider this: Queen Victoria's beloved Prince Consort, Albert, found himself attacked as part of the British media's Russophobia at the time of the Crimean crisis (although he was German, the press drew little distinction between the two nationalities). It went so far that he was accused of treason and one newspaper called for his execution, adding for good measure: "Better that a few drops of guilty blood should be shed on a scaffold on Tower Hill than that a country should be baulked of its desire for war!" Queen Victoria was so outraged that she threatened to abdicate, Figes writes, but it had little impact on newspaper editors, because such talk sold newspapers.

The Crimean War reminds us that many of the things we tend to see as unprecedented in our debates about politics and the media are not new at all: certainly not politicians playing with defence and national security, and certainly not the media taking aggressive, jingoistic and partisan positions. In fact, given the interwoven history of newspapers and political pamphlets, it is more accurate to see the recent decades, when journalism was seen to aspire – at its more serious end – to sober, investigative and responsible reporting, as an aberration.

What is new is that business pressures and technological changes have coincided with a renewed shrillness. This means double trouble for any hope that the media will fulfil their role to document events fully and fairly, and so write the first draft of history.

The media should remain a major repository of our collective memory. Just as historians go to old newspapers to gain a sense of what people were talking about, what views they held and how politicians responded, people still rely on the media to tell them what is going on today. Yet forced to generate 24-hour-a-day news, and under intense financial pressure, the media struggle to retain their own memory of what has gone before, and – if they do keep it – the capacity to set a story in any longer-term context. The need for the new means the media increasingly work in the "present tense." They can only frame events by what is happening contemporaneously. The rise of the trivial story that erupts and then disappears, and the tendency to see events purely for how they affect individual players in that particular story – rather than their longer-term implications – start to become inevitable. The opportunities also dwindle to go back and review what happened after the initial flurry of interest in a story abates.

The speed with which we can obtain new information changes the context in which we see it. We now perpetually update stories with the incremental addition of new facts. The time – only a couple of years ago – when print deadlines on newspapers effectively pressed "pause" on a view of history is gone. Now when editors ask journalists for stories for the morning print edition, they do so having absorbed and often discarded – as "old news" – events reported on the web that day. They want the "throw-forward" story, or the completely new fact or idea that will survive twelve hours of print turnaround time.

It is little wonder that, amid all this noise, editors – even before they look to advance an ideological or commercial agenda – seek to re-assert their influence by declaring an issue a national emergency or seeking notoriety through inflammatory comment.

This is not a purely Australian phenomenon, of course. Matt Bai covered three presidential campaigns for the *New York Times Magazine*. Last year he published a book on what would seem an unlikely subject of interest to Australian political junkies: the downfall of Gary Hart, a frontrunner for the Democratic presidential nomination in 1987 until he was undone by a story about a frolic with a beautiful young blonde on a boat with the unfortunate name of *Monkey Business*. The book is not just about what happened to Hart. In *All the Truth Is Out: The Week Politics Went Tabloid*, Bai looks at the conjunction of changes that made Hart's scandal a turning point in the way politics is covered in America. Thankfully, we haven't seen all of these trends in Australia – the media here are more cautious about entering politicians' private lives – but the overwhelming majority are painfully familiar: the way it has become always about throwing forward, always about personality. Bai describes how Hart was hit in 1987 by "all these disparate, emerging forces in the society – a vacuum in the political debate, changing ideas about morality, a new generational ethos and new technologies in the media, [and] the tabloidization of every aspect of American life."

By 1987, the 24/7 news cycle was well underway with the rise and rise of CNN, itself built on new technologies of easily transportable satellite dishes and the switch from film to video. There was also the stripping down of borders of news with the arrival of the fax machine. The age when most Americans only read their local newspaper and there was a diversity of coverage was starting to fade as newspapers could get instant readouts of what papers in other parts of the country were reporting.

For those interested in the machinations of the media, a particularly fascinating aspect of the Gary Hart scandal was that the story was broken by the *Miami Herald*, which had staked out Hart's townhouse in Washington. Until then, national politics in the United States had been largely reported by White House correspondents and was the preserve of big mastheads, such as the *New York Times* and *Washington Post*. Two non–White House reporters for the *Post* broke the Watergate story in the 1970s, but other newspapers didn't poke their noses much into Washington politics. You can imagine the humiliation for the Washington media establishment when the *Miami Herald* broke a story that happened on its own patch. The press corps had also always kept out of politicians' personal lives, and particularly those of presidents. Bai argues that the culture of journalism, and of American journalists seeing themselves as having to, above all else, uncover politicians' lies, started over guilt that they'd missed the Watergate story. It caused everyone to try to be Woodward and Bernstein. And then it morphed into a complete monster as the barriers to reporting politics were smashed and the job was taken out of the hands of the Washington elites: "Politicians were now fair game for all the media, just as it was going tabloid in all facets of society."

At the same time, the vast expanse of 24-hour news meant reporters suddenly found new identities as celebrities and commentators on panel discussion shows. "Little wonder politicians became defensive and little wonder – crucially – that the relationships between journalists and politicians changed dramatically."

> What made political journalism so alluring, so important, was the idea that you actually got to know the minds of the public servants you were writing about. You were supposed to share beers at the

hotel bar and late-night confidences aboard the chartered plane. You were supposed to understand not just the candidates' policy papers or their strategies for winning but also what made them good and worthy of trust or what didn't.

However,

> by the time my contemporaries and I got there ... presidential politics – indeed, all of politics – was really nothing like that. With rare exceptions, our cautious candidates were like smiling holograms programmed to speak and smile but not to interact, so that it sometimes seemed you could run your hand through them ... Candidates in the age of Oprah "shared" more than ever before, but what they shared of themselves – boxers rather than briefs, allusions to youthful drug use – was trivial and often rehearsed, as authentic as a piece of plastic fruit, and about as illuminating.

Bai relates what happened when he gained an interview with John Kerry during the 2004 presidential campaign. He "assumed Kerry would welcome the opportunity to elaborate on his actual plan for governing, rather than having to answer yet more questions about the authenticity of his war medals" but in fact "he seemed to regard me not as someone who sought to explain his views (which is how I saw myself) but rather as a hired assassin who had just walked through the front door without so much as a struggle."

Bai's book nails why political journalism operates the way it does in Australia these days. It is helpful – as is the reminder from the distant Crimean War that a partisan media is hardly a new phenomenon – in unpacking structural trends in Australian journalism that can get drowned out in the local angst about what has happened to News Corp and Fairfax.

Whatever job we do, we are inclined to respond, like Pavlov's dog, to incentives. The rewards for political journalists in Australia – whether in the form of promotion, notoriety on social media, or becoming a "commentator" – flow when you have an "exclusive," when you write the supposed "inside story," or particularly when you write punchy commentary. They rarely come from spending a couple of days getting to grips with a policy debate and explaining to readers the pros and cons of outcomes – if indeed you can get such a piece in the paper at all. You might get away with talking about the cost to the budget. But you will be rewarded most if you write about how it affects the political fortunes of the two sides of politics. In a world where there are fewer and fewer bodies in the newsroom, and there is greater and greater demand to punch out stories, your chances of having enough time to do that work are minimal, but you will always be able to get a yarn in the paper if it goes to the political contest. We tend to think that this is just because in-depth policy stories are a little too "worthy," that they are not "sexy" – and there's something to that. But we have also fallen out of the habit of seeing a role for such reporting because no one has the time to do it. Over time, it's become a forgotten skill.

The days of specialist reporters in the Canberra press gallery – reporters who would cover education, welfare or health, for example – are long gone. Instead of reporters who cover issues day in, day out as they develop, we have generalists. The generalists descend on the story of the day, whatever the policy area, and have to make instant sense of it. How many people do they know who are experts on the subject, or even experts on the politics of the subject? Where are they going to start but at the point of political contention? What is the easiest thing to report but the mechanics of the political brawl, rather than the substance of the matter being brawled over?

Without an obligation, or opportunity, to know the history of an issue, it is natural that journalists will make the context of reporting the issues – and politics – of the day. But that only increases a tendency to see the story in black-and-white terms. They have no time to consider that a debate about the subject at hand might, or even should be allowed to, develop. And they are even more unlikely to follow it up to see what happens tomorrow, because they will have been forced to move on to the next issue.

On any given day, a generalist reporter will cover the issue of the day, whether that be (some recent examples) a summit between political leaders and indigenous leaders on reform of the constitution, the restructuring of a $20 billion agreement between the government and the pharmaceutical industry that determines how much we pay for our drugs at the chemist, or (those perennials) tax reform and reform of the federation.

In the press gallery, I estimate there have been four or five "generations" of journalists (there is a turnover every two or three years) who do not remember a time when political stories were not framed as leadership stories, or took as their focus how a policy decision would affect the fortunes of the major political parties, rather than giving at least some consideration to whether it is a good or bad policy, and how it might affect voters.

Relationships between the media and politicians have also changed. Politics is no longer the exclusive preserve of a few press gallery journalists. Politicians must deal with journalists right across the country. That is fine, except that with it goes the capacity – or need – to form trusting relationships with journalists which might allow politicians to feel confident thinking out loud about the options they have in front of them, or explaining how their thinking about an issue has developed. Politicians here are likely to identify with John Kerry in seeing Matt Bai as a hired assassin. The likelihood that one group of journalists will directly report on, or even talk to politicians about, any particular issue for more than a day at a time is now remote.

Social media and the internet have broken down the "barriers to entry" to the media, thereby allowing a massive amount of material to be presented. The benefit is that experts in a particular field can get their views heard quickly. (Look at the success of a site like *The Conversation*, part-funded by the universities.) But social media do not have as much access to the people and institutions that drive our system as the traditional media do, even if relations between the media and politicians have deteriorated. They don't get the chance to question, or to interact. Social media commentary is framed as if looking in through a window.

Major reports and factual data that people could once have accessed only through the media are now available on the internet. Such access is a good thing, but the sheer volume of material may mean that even fewer people see it. And the media are no longer always in a position to synthesise it for them with any real expertise.

These changes have come about – and helped drive – a very different interaction between the media and politicians to that of the past. It lies at the heart of an inanity that drives voters to despair.

But I should also defend the press gallery. Having endured countless rants over the years about how dreadful the gallery is, how it engages in groupthink, I find it ironic that the quality of political coverage has become much worse as technology has freed both politicians and journalists from the constraints of Canberra. Critics of the press gallery often excoriate journalists – and particularly commentators – who don't work in it, and in fact have never worked as political journalists. And while many on social media rail against the influence and narrow view of the "MSM" (mainstream media), the great irony is that much of the conversation on social media is much more partisan – in both directions – than anything you will see in a newspaper.

As politicians have become less likely to share late-night confidences with journalists and commentators, the appetite for the "inside story" has only grown. Yet, as Matt Bai also observes, the inside stories are too often nothing of the sort. When Cheryl Kernot defected from the Democrats to Labor in 1998, newspapers immediately wanted the inside story of this stunning political shift of allegiance. It really had come out of the blue, so by the time reporters went in search of what had happened, anyone with the slightest connection to it was in lockdown. Eventually we were all called down, one or two at a time, to Gareth Evans' office, where he told us how the deal with Kernot had been done over a plunger of coffee. Was it only me who was mortified the next morning to see that same plunger of coffee anecdote spread across every paper in the country? It was the beginning of the formulaic "inside story" (and of course it was later revealed that the story was more complicated than first appeared).

The formulas are never thicker on the ground than they are at the time of the federal budget, partly because the budget lock-up and the sheer volume of copy mean newspapers – and electronic media – have to plan how coverage is going to be structured days, if not weeks, in advance and hope like mad there will be no huge surprises which require changes not just to specific content, but to the overall coverage. There are stories allocated by area – health, defence, education. There are set budget and economic stories. There are pre-arranged "cameos" to illustrate how the budget affects particular groups. In Canberra, there are the set interviews with the treasurer a few days before the budget, which one hopes contain some tiny new fact. There is the Sunday television interview to set the government's political message.

Amid this planning and massaging, all the pre-budget commentary disappears and the entire conversation about the state of the government's books is restarted. In part that is necessary, because there are new forecasts and an entire new round of spending and tax measures to be debated. But between the pre-planning and the formulas, discussions which relate the budget to everything that went before are largely lost. Before a budget, for example, the talk may have been all about the need to rein in spending. After a budget, a massive tax cut that wasn't expected dominates not just the headlines but also the debate as a whole. All the talk about reining in spending disappears. Similarly, budgets are assessed for what they mean for the government – and the treasurer – and for whether they are politically "smart" or not, rather than for whether they are good or bad for the country.

There has been much angst at the blatant recent attempts at political influence by news organisations or individual broadcasters. If there was a deep, deep irony in Malcolm Turnbull's toppling of Tony Abbott in 2014, however, it was that a tweet in support of Abbott by Rupert Murdoch, and a story about a front-bench reshuffle leaked to News Corp's *Daily Telegraph*, which was probably supposed to be helpful to the government, were two of the final straws for Abbott's prime ministership. They both convinced the plotters that they had to move sooner rather than later.

I believe that the way the media are losing their memory and no longer providing a reliable contemporary record is more insidiously dangerous for our politics than the attempt by some in the press to become political players.

There was much that was jingoistic in the coverage of the Crimean War – reports of the Charge of the Light Brigade comes to mind. But the reporting of the suffering of the troops transformed the medical care of armies, and ultimately the work of nursing, as represented by the figure of Florence Nightingale. One wonders whether, in the modern era, the Charge and the Lady with the Lamp might have done no more than briefly flare in the 24-hour news cycle and then vanish. Would the Charge have become famous without footage of it? Would journalists keep on the case of unsanitary conditions in military hospitals?

Changing technology too often traps the media in the present tense, yet it also provides a new, almost infinite space in which to give readers all the background and context they need to understand events. But for these links to consist of more than just the standard time-lines and quotes will require a memory of what has gone before – not only a memory of events, but also one which tells us how things were once done differently and, as a result, how they might be done differently again.

LEARNING TO REMEMBER

Two thousand years ago, Tacitus painted a chilling picture of the transition from the Roman Republic to the Roman Empire. It was chilling because it depicted in just a few phrases how the combination of personal will, the destruction or decline of Rome's institutions of power, and a population prepared to forget the past and make the most of a new political order cleared the way for a profound transformation of one of the world's great civilisations.

We often wonder how societies allow themselves to be led into war or dictatorship. Often such things emerge from other crises and sources of misery. But at some point – as happened to Tacitus's Romans – it becomes easier to accept the present than to yearn for a past before things went bad. And the present envelops societies all the faster if they don't understand or remember what has gone before.

I'm not suggesting for a moment that we are on the edge of such a precipice. But I am pointing out that the institutions which have made Australia's political system so vibrant and successful have been changing profoundly over the past few decades. These changes include the rise of an unstable executive government (because it has lost the capacity to build institutional memory) at the cost of the parliament (which has also lost its memory as it struggles for relevance); the decline in the influence of the public sector (as a result of a range of forces which have robbed it of much of its institutional memory); the relative rise of the national security establishment (which maintains its influence and its memory); and the transformation of the media into a channel for present-tense information, rather than a reliable repository of the historic record. In the background there has also been a steady nibbling away at our civil rights, as relentless incremental change has left many of us unaware how far the law has moved in the past couple of decades.

Australia was a pioneer in the ways of politics and governance at the time of federation. We fancied ourselves a workingman's paradise and valued the power of law and government to shape society through industrial relations and wage-setting, and the protection of particular industries. That gave us a particularly strong set of expectations about the way the country worked, and the role of government in this. But it also gave us, over time, an exceptionally strong set of institutions – from stable government (which at different times has been boringly unadventurous and profoundly innovative) to a vibrant parliament and a public sector made influential by world war and rapid national expansion.

The past few decades have seen a waning of much of the powerful government influence on our lives. That is not necessarily a bad thing. Nothing I have written here is a nostalgic lament, a plea to go back to the good old days. But with that waning have also gone memories and really deep understandings of how things were done in the past. We have reached the point where there isn't a widespread recognition of just how much this political amnesia affects what we know and understand about our country, and what has been involved in making it tick.

We talk endlessly about how Australia needs to lift its game, how things need to change for progress to occur. But the conversation is perpetually narrowed and burdened by being framed as a series of character assessments of our leaders, as if one individual can determine our fate. I argue that the steady decline in our collective institutional memory is having a profound impact on the quality of our political and policy debate. While we talk endlessly about what needs to change, we don't stop to consider what has already changed and the unintended consequences of this – the shifts in the nature, effectiveness and relative power of our institutions of government.

*

Tony Abbott won office in 2013 on a platform of undoing things: reversing specific measures like the "carbon tax," but also removing the sense of chaos which voters felt surrounded the Gillard government. Apparently more by accident than design, Abbott then proceeded to do the reverse of everything he had promised: he didn't keep his word about the budget, and he ran a government which couldn't persuade voters that it was in control of things. Not only that, voters were alarmed and confused by the person they found occupying the prime minister's office and the messages that his actions sent out: the flags at press conferences, the knighthoods, the assent to legal racial bigotry.

More than that, Abbott revealed a surprising lack of political dexterity. He could not adjust his tactics or his thinking to the times. He "closed down" to a binary world of black and white. In political terms, you were either on Team Australia, or not. Well before the events of September 2015, two particular incidents turned the tide irrevocably for the former prime minister. Abbott's attempt to steamroll his cabinet on stripping citizenship rights from terrorists forced six ministers to break spectacularly with their leader. His attempt to steamroll the Liberal Party room on marriage equality – by insisting it was an issue that needed to be considered by the joint party room, where Nationals' votes would support his position – was equally fatal. Both moves went a step too far in challenging the political structures of government.

A black-and-white world sees many issues pushed "off the table" – not through fear, but because of the sense that there is no point discussing things that will not be countenanced by the powers that be. If we are thinking in black-and-white terms, we are not consulting our memories of what has happened in the past, but instead reacting purely to current events and to ideology. We don't talk about the need for an overall change to the tax mix, for example, because politicians or interest groups have ruled out changing the GST. We don't contemplate modification of our border-protection or asylum-seeker policies – even at the margins – because the policy has been declared and is unalterable. We can't have a rational conversation about industrial relations because one side of politics simplifies it to an attack on workers and the other side finds it politically dangerous.

Beyond a penchant for black-and-white thinking, Tony Abbott's greatest sin may have been his remorseless degradation of our political institutions. Abbott's failure to run a successful cabinet government, his disdain for parliamentary negotiation and his undercutting of the public service were all the more perplexing given his avowed conservatism. As a "true conservative," he might have been expected to feel an affinity for our institutional history, for the way things were done in the past.

That is why the significance of the shift to Malcolm Turnbull is potentially much deeper than the outcome of the next election. Tony Abbott didn't just (try to) shut down dissent in his own ranks. He sent out a message of deep distrust of the public service. It started with the sacking of four department heads, but continued through, as far as many other senior bureaucrats were concerned, to the way he dealt with them. There were persistent attacks on institutions like the ABC, the Human Rights Commission and "activist" courts, yet a constant drumbeat of approval for anything to do with the military. Abbott was not the first prime minister to erode the standing of our institutions, but he was one of the most aggressive.

What the new prime minister has said he aims to do is to restore not just proper cabinet processes but a system of consultation to elicit the expertise that may lie within executive government. We might see this as a mere matter of "process," but it is implicitly much more than that. Ministers, under this system, are assumed to know a lot more of the history of an issue than the prime minister's office, and it should be they who advise their colleagues on the best course of action. By definition, this diffusion of power should foster more internal debate on policy. Debate relies on a more complex set of arguments, which requires the debaters to go in search of information, including examples from history, to back up their case. Turnbull has brought into the centre of the government people with a memory of how the executive worked under John Howard. Public servants are returning to ministers' offices as chiefs of staff and ministerial advisers in greater numbers. Turnbull has immediately engaged with the Senate crossbench. His ministers have opened pragmatic negotiations with Labor to achieve compromises that had been flatly ruled out under the previous leader. The new prime minister has gone to great pains to re-engage the public service in government. Well before he became leader, he recognised it as an institution that needed to be nurtured. "There's no single answer to this but managing a talented workforce is very, very hard." he said in June. "You're in the talent business. The talent is the real asset of the Australian Public Service, so we have got to have a focus on the APS, a respect for the quality and seek to promote and improve the quality of that workforce all the time."

These are the fine intentions, anyway. We have yet to see whether, in the hothouse and hurly-burly of politics, Turnbull can start the long turnaround in the way our political institutions work. It is hard to change habits, particularly when you are in a hurry. And it is particularly hard when people don't remember that things can be done differently.

And in any case, it would be a huge mistake to see what is happening only in the immediate context of the shift from Abbott to Turnbull – to think that Malcolm Turnbull's pledges to change the way government works could reverse all the crumbling of our institutions of several decades. The changes to executive government – as documented in this essay – stretch all the way back to the Whitlam years. Turnbull is effectively promising to leapfrog back over Abbott, Gillard and Rudd to the last time it seemed to work well. The questions we can't answer yet are whether Turnbull's methods will produce better results than those of his immediate predecessors, or whether other factors – notably technology, or the changing nature of the issues now on the federal agenda – mean the old system is well and truly broken. The very deterioration in the way our institutions have operated in the past eight years – the loss of memory in the public service, in the parliament and within the ministerial wing of Parliament House – may also hinder the new regime.

One of the big changes is not in what the prime minister does, but in how his cabinet behaves. It was Howard who ushered in the era of the permanent campaign. Thinking elections all the time has a profound impact on the way politicians act. Everything becomes (even more) political, obviously. But the idea that an election campaign may be only months away – because a minority government may collapse, because a double-dissolution election may be called – imposes a discipline on a parliamentary party that might otherwise not exist.

The tight discipline of the Rudd-led Opposition and then the Abbott-led Opposition produced a culture that, from the outside, seemed much too subservient to the leader, lest any perceived division become a matter of political controversy. Unfortunately, having established that culture, that memory of how things were done, it was very difficult to break with it in government. Yet the events of the past two years have forced the Coalition front bench to reconsider. Ministers now acknowledge the need for a truly collegiate, cabinet-based government. That is, it is not just the prime minister who has to change, but ministers too, in how they conceive of their role and assert their influence. The departure of many of those on the front bench during the Rudd–Gillard years – and much soul-searching within Labor ranks – is also producing a more feisty internal debate in the Opposition. If there is indeed a successful transition back to cabinet-style government, this will form the core of a new set of institutional memories for both sides of politics.

Yet politics is a transitory business. Writing about the traits and trends of the forty-third parliament at the end of 2013, Martin Lumb of the Parliamentary Library noted:

> As at 1 July 2011, of the 226 members of the 43rd Parliament, nearly two-thirds (148 MPs or 65 per cent) had served less than 12 years; 45 members (20 per cent) had served less than three years.

It only takes a couple of elections for a considerable amount of the parliament's working memory to disappear. Consider, for example, how few MPs would have direct experience of all the shifts in national security legislation that have taken place since 9/11. The number of really long-serving MPs and senators – particularly those who have been ministers –

is dropping. You peak in your career as a minister, and then you get out. (Some argue this is one of the side effects of changes to parliamentary superannuation.) Former ministers are useful not only to their parties, but also to the parliament as a whole, with many long-serving MPs sitting on committees dealing with their old portfolios and able to enlighten new members on past considerations. Clare O'Neil and Tim Watts, young Labor MPs who published a book, Two Futures, in 2015, observed that:

> Rapid turnover of leaders is not intrinsically negative. Like the directors of companies or other organisations, political leaders must be accountable to the system that elects them. There are some countries where leaders hold power for decades unchallenged, and this can reflect a failure of accountability. But, at the same time, the pace of turnover of political leadership has real costs for our democracy ... These days, former leaders will often quickly leave parliament. New generations of parliamentarians must learn the lessons of politics without the benefits of on-the-job mentoring.

O'Neil and Watts also propose in their book that we should consider some radical uses of technology to make parliament more relevant. They suggest a proportion of every parliamentary sitting week be dedicated to citizens' business, "in which Australian citizens directly propose topics for debate by their elected representatives." They note that the Finnish parliament requires a parliamentary debate and a vote on:

> the substance of any motion that attracts more than fifty thousand online signatures. A platform that enables Australians to vote online to determine the issues that their MPs debate would give parliamentarians direct feedback about the strength of community sentiment on particular issues, and give citizens concerned about those issues the satisfaction that their parliament was engaging with them.

There's a lot more, too, on radical reform of Question Time, even moving it to prime viewing time as a way to put more pressure on MPs to behave.

The key thing, as I see it, is to revive the institution of the parliament. If MPs once again see it as a powerful platform, that will only increase their desire to become not just good politicians, but good parliamentarians.

The extent to which we seem to have forgotten what our parliament is for can be illustrated by the fact that more than once in the past five years the idea has been floated that a "citizens' assembly" should get together to discuss a particular issue. When Julia Gillard suggested it in 2010, she was rightly ridiculed by those who pointed out the parliament was, in fact, a citizens' assembly. It reflects how little confidence the broader community has in the parliament as a representative community body – and one capable of capturing a multiplicity of views – that the suggestion keeps arising.

*

At an event to support Andrew Hastie, the Liberal candidate in the 2015 Canning by-election, Tony Abbott introduced two of his colleagues by their military titles. Hastie himself is a decorated former army officer. A political strategist commented at the time on the increased number of defence personnel entering politics. Whatever the merits of the individual candidate, he observed, the thing that political parties find attractive about military people is that their pitch to voters is credible and straightforward. It is taken as read that they want to serve their country, so awkward questions are unlikely to arise about their motivations or professional background. Equally, in polls asking respondents to rate different professions, nurses and police are invariably near the top of the list. People in these professions are overwhelmingly public servants. Public servants as a category in their own right also rate pretty highly – certainly higher than either politicians or journalists.

Drop the term "public servant" into a political debate at the tabloid end of the discussion, though, and they become "fat cats" and purveyors of red tape. And in discussions about reforming the economy, the public sector is generally seen as a negative. The loss of public service jobs is viewed as a sign of government fiscal machismo, or just a necessary outcome of reducing the drag on the economy. If large companies go through a major restructure, they set aside significant resources to oversee the change and bed it down. Yet in the public service, large swathes of the bureaucracy can be moved from minister to minister, as portfolios are sliced up, then re-sliced to appease the ambitions, egos or whims of members of the government. Whole areas of administration and policy can be moved from department to department, sometimes twice in a year, with no allowance made for the disruption. Instead, there are jokes about having to change the letterhead again.

All things considered, we seem to have developed a very confused view of public servants, the public service and even the public sector. We laud our military and its actions. We approve of public servants like nurses and policemen. But we speak disparagingly of public servants who might advise governments, and we presume that the private sector always knows best.

Yet is the private sector really that different? Writing in the *Harvard Business Review* in 2013, the business consultant Ron Ashkenas reflected on returning to a large corporation – where he had consulted on a specific issue years earlier – and finding to his astonishment that he was seen as one of the corporation's "main repositories of institutional memory." He added that, "Although this is an extreme example, it's not unique." His advice was to "build an explicit strategy for maintaining institutional memory, even in your own team":

> Don't assume that it will happen by itself ... [and] use technology
> to create a process by which your team continually captures and
> curates institutional knowledge – to make it a living and evolving
> body of useful information that is accessible to people as they
> come into the organization. In this day and age of Alzheimer's Dis-
> ease and dementia, everyone knows that an individual's memory
> is fragile. What we often don't recognize is that organizational

memory is much the same – and if we don't actively preserve it, we put ourselves at risk.

If the government wants to take advice from the private sector – and particularly from consultants – then perhaps Ashkenas's advice about maintaining institutional memory should be at the top of the list.

Executive government – that is, the ministry – and parliamentary parties need to put serious thought into how best to preserve their institutional memory as the cast of individual ministers and staff turns over at an accelerating pace. The best thing that they can do is to understand what has happened to the capabilities of the public service already, and consider not just how to rebuild it, but also that the way it has been used by politicians over the past few decades has led to decline.

It is in the inner sanctums of the political system that the public service seems to have lost most status in recent times. The disdain of the Abbott era effectively closed off, outside the areas of national security and foreign affairs, much of this important repository of policy advice and memory from the Coalition government. But it was a process that had been underway for some time.

Merely being nicer to the public service is clearly not enough to remedy several decades of decline. The complex reasons for this alienation of executive government from the public service – which, as we have seen, goes well beyond simple politicisation – make it a hard thing to unwind. It's also not just about the public servants, of course. The broader question is what we expect the public sector to do for us these days: whether we are happy with the current mish-mash of public and private providers, with its implications for accountability and transparency; and whether we have to rethink the idea that, in all things, the private sector does a better job.

We have to consider what the core work of the public service is, or – alternatively – what should not go into the hands of the private sector. That covers everything from whether it is appropriate for people detained in the government's name – and therefore in its care – to be policed by private contractors, to the question of ownership and protection of data gathered by the government. If government *were* a private company, the board would be likely to try to define what the core business of that company is; what its core assets are. In the modern world, where data is the most valuable commodity, a company's database would be its core asset. It would also be the institutional memory tied up in its people.

As prime minister, Tony Abbott would say that governments should only do for citizens what they cannot do for themselves. He defined that very narrowly. Defence is the classic example. Yet most of us know very little about what has happened to our defence and national security institutions in the last twenty years. In a paper published in 2014, the former Labor senator and defence minister John Faulkner noted that in the period since 9/11, "the size of Australia's intelligence organisations and their budgets have more than tripled." For example, ASIO's staff grew from 565 in 1999 to 1792 in 2013. Its budget expanded commensurately from \$65.7 million in 1999–2000 to \$443.8 million in 2013–14. Furthermore, Faulkner writes:

> A significant volume of legislation passed through the Parliament has given the intelligence agencies and other security agencies including the AFP unprecedented powers. These new laws included: new terrorism offences with a broader definition of terrorism, terrorist acts and terrorist organisations; laws prohibiting the financing of terrorism or receiving funds from a terrorist organisation; laws against advocating or praising terrorism, associating with terrorist organisations or recruiting for terrorist organisations or giving support to a terrorist organisation.

While we are only vaguely aware of the growing power of one arm of government, we are kidding ourselves about our continuing commitment to provide services to many Australians who cannot provide for themselves. The delivery of these services has become "invisible" to us because it has been contracted out. We cannot properly assess whether the people who need these services are getting them, whether the services are of a sufficient quality, or whether they represent value for money.

In the narrower but crucial world of policy advice, there has never been a greater need for intellectual firepower, and for a deep memory. In their time, the Seven Dwarfs were able to mobilise the forces of government and facilitate a massive expansion of Australia's population and industrial base. No one is suggesting that is the right response now, but a capacity to respond to the circumstances of the day is always necessary. In the history wars between the Coalition and Labor over which had the biggest impact in the 1980s and 1990s, both sides seem to have forgotten that the best periods of reform were collaborative creations: there was real but productive tension between politicians and policy-makers, with each bringing the memory and experience of their respective realms to the discussion.

Now we have a public sector from which much expertise has been lost. Change has left the public service as both piggy in the middle and a rabbit in the headlights (to mix my metaphors). Public servants find themselves shoved into the public arena to defend decisions that their political masters have made, although they often had little input in the original decision, nor do they have any direct way of controlling its implementation by contracted parties. It is not just Senate committee hearings that leave public servants feeling vulnerable.

The one thing the public service could offer in this dangerous world where it has neither responsibility for final decisions nor the direct capacity to carry them out is the memory of how government dealt with problems in the past, and how and why it took the decisions it did. But advice usually means a paper trail. A senior public servant says that an unintended consequence of freedom-of-information laws has been to create a culture in which public servants "don't want to write advice down." "You can't have private conversations anymore," one says, lest the advice turn up in an FOI request which leaves public servants, rather than their political masters, accountable for decisions that they have not taken.

Rebuilding policy capability requires lowering the risk public servants face in giving advice. It may also involve changing recruitment and promotion so that those who build up long-term memory in a particular area are not effectively penalised for it. And it may mean rebuilding the wider culture. "What can be done to ensure good people enter public service?" a senior public servant says. "One word: respect. If you disparage an institution over a long enough period, you will slowly but surely undercut the quality of people who want to go there. And respect is different from being free from criticism."

It should be noted that many of our most senior bureaucrats also think that the public sector has to toughen up and stop being quite so cowed by the rise of executive government. Michael Thawley, as the secretary of PM&C, is the titular head of the public service. He told a conference in Canberra in September:

> We're not just here to write papers, elegant or otherwise ... We're actually here to ensure that things change. It's no use us shrugging our shoulders if the government doesn't accept our very wise suggestions about how to reform this or the other thing. Why did we fail to convince the government to do what we suggested? ... Did we fail to provide adequate evidence? Were we unpersuasive? Did we not talk to the various stakeholders? ... Did we talk enough to people outside the system generally?

Don Russell says much the same thing:

> The wise [departmental] Secretary realises early on that advice to Ministers is contestable. If departmental advice is to have influence, it has to be useful. It is a mistake to think that the department's main influence comes from creating the piece of paper that cannot be ignored. It is true that you should never underestimate the power of the written word, but if the department is only viewed as having a capacity to hem in a minister, then over time the department will

find itself frozen out and more and more decisions will be taken late at night in ministers' offices.

The missing ingredient that holds back departmental advice is imagination. We have to create an APS where departments become ideas factories; ideas that have been properly researched and tested and that are only looking for objectives and values to be harnessed by the minister or government of the day.

Ministers should take advice from their departments not because they have to but because they want to.

Still another says:

Sure, there is the capacity for advisers to be bastards. But the onus is on the public service to stand up to that. The public service has become very weak.

It's not that the public service and politicians aren't aware of these problems. It's rather that until things came to a head under Tony Abbott, they didn't receive concerted attention. They were just part of an ongoing downward spiral. There are signs here and there that the public service is trying to rebuild its memory banks. One example is the decision to have the head of PM&C, and the head of the NSW Department of Premier and Cabinet, review what happened in dealings with the Lindt Café killer, Man Haron Monis. If officials were to learn something from this tragedy, the thinking went, they needed to be exposed directly to what had happened and consider where they had gone wrong.

In some cases, politicians and public servants are also thinking twice before automatically contracting out policy or review work to consultants. It is revealing when one public servant observes that contracting out "is the easy path when you don't have any ideas and are looking for new ones." "Besides," he says, "the outside consultant's report tends to be seen as having more credibility."

These are very small steps. Not everyone in the public service or politics is exercised by the need for change, nor do they see it as a priority when they are caught up dealing with the crisis of the day. And politicians still pander to an insatiable media by seeking to have something "new" or "announceable" to offer every day.

Rapidly evolving media technology is not just changing the way we do things, it is changing the way we think about them. We have access to an unprecedented amount of material, yet the sheer volume militates against the capacity to absorb and synthesise it. Developing a "narrative" that can be maintained over months which is about ideas rather than new verbs is difficult.

The American educationalist Mark Prensky set off a hot debate fifteen years ago when he coined the term "digital native" to talk about the problems educators had engaging students when the young were more at home with new technology than their teachers. While the debate about digital natives has many aspects, its implication for how young people think about things is something that exercises some of our younger MPs, like Labor's Ed Husic: the idea that young people process information very differently; and that they may have too few opportunities to absorb and analyse – let alone remember – what they see and hear. For politicians, part of the difficulty of "feeding the beast," and getting your message out, is that readers and viewers can now be highly selective about what they consume.

If the force for change thirty years ago was the need to make the economy internationally competitive, whether we liked it or not, the force today is technology, whether we are ready for it or not. The central dilemma is that technology, if anything, is acting against institutional memory. Yet the sheer bombardment of information technology only increases the need to think about how best to safeguard it.

*

My *AFR* colleague Phil Coorey sometimes yells out across the office to me: "Oi! Yesteryear correspondent, when did [such and such event] happen?" At some point in the past ten years, I became the veteran staffer who is consulted on "ancient" history. We are products of our time, and our views of the world are formed accordingly. My professional career began with the 1980s and coincided with a dramatic new era in politics and policy debate. All that has happened in the following thirty-five years has shaped the way I see politics. Sometimes you realise with a rude shock that all the stuff you carry around every day in your head isn't in everyone else's head.

This came home to me most powerfully in 2012, when I was doing interviews to discuss my first Quarterly Essay. Before we started the formal interview, a radio journalist warned: "Oh, by the way, don't presume too much political memory in the audience." "Sure," I said, "what shouldn't I presume they know?" "Well, don't presume they will know who Paul Keating is, or what he did." I concede this caused a sharp intake of breath on my part. Yes, it was a youngish audience, but a politically articulate one. How could they not know who Paul Keating was? He had been one of our prime ministers, for goodness sake. Then I thought again. There had been three prime ministers since Keating left office in 1996. Anyone aged under thirty would have no adult memory of government before John Howard. The views of these people are just as relevant as mine. But they will be shaped by a very different set of memories.

How many of us actually remember some of the changes in politics, public policy and the public service that I've discussed in this essay? How many are aware, for example, of the changes in indigenous affairs of the past twenty years?

While we may refer knowingly to the first budget of the Howard government as a vehicle which set up spectacular political success for the Coalition, how many of us remember the decisions taken in that budget? How many people recall that the budget's political success was partly built on the spectacular misjudgments of its opponents: the trade unions who violently stormed Parliament House and caused a public backlash, which helped quell immediate political opposition to the budget? How many people remember that the day the budget was brought down was the day the deal was announced to give a Labor "rat," Mal Colston, the Senate deputy presidency and thus make the Senate a much more compliant upper house?

Even though ministers in Tony Abbott's government believed that in the 2014 budget they were replicating Howard's modus operandi, it turned out that their memories were faulty. The structures they put in place, the lack of experience of the staff they had in their offices and their failure to remember the other factors that ultimately allowed the 1996 budget to be a political success made that replication impossible.

*

During the 1990s, then Russian prime minister Viktor Chernomyrdin became notorious for his malapropisms and endearing turns of phrase. There was something wonderfully and absurdly bureaucratic about many of these expressions, such as "We have completed all the items: from A to B," "The principles that were principled were non-principled," and "There is still time to save the face. Later we will be forced to save some other parts of a body." Perhaps most famously, he declared that "Whatever organisation we try to create, it always ends up looking like the Communist Party."

My favourite among his declarations, though, is: "It has never been like this and now it is exactly the same again." In the process of remaking our economy, and in the wake of a technological revolution, we have sometimes unwittingly remade our political institutions. They are not serving us well because they don't remember how things were done in the past. The risk isn't that we will end up in exactly the same place again, but that we will end up somewhere else quite unintended.

It is time to start learning to remember.

ACKNOWLEDGMENTS AND SOURCES

For Tosca Ramsey, *diva filia*

"venimus, vidimus, prandimus ...
forsan et haec olim meninisse iuvabit"

1–2   "When after the destruction" and "when Pompeius was": Tacitus, *The Annals*, Book I, 1.2.

9   "seeing health, education" and "These areas are": Pradeep Philip, speech delivered to the Trans-Tasman Business Circle in Melbourne, 28 July 2015.

9   "Public servants": John Stone, quoted in *Age*, 25 November 1982.

11   "I think many": Ken Henry to author, June 2015.

11   "The blurring of boundaries": Martin Parkinson to author, July 2015.

14–15 "Progress, far from" and "Fanaticism consists": George Santayana, *Reason in Common Sense*, Volume 1 of *The Life of Reason*, 1905–06.

18   "'the new mandarins'" and subsequent quotes: Nicholas Brown, *The Seven Dwarfs and the Age of the Mandarins*, Australian National University Press, 2015.

19–20 "The Prime Minister of the day" and subsequent quotes: Don Russell, *Reflections on My Time in Canberra*, Crawford School lecture, 31 March 2014.

21   "A detailed secret brief": Interview with Hawke era official, September 2015.

21–2 "I want a strong" and "The situation was": Paul Kelly, *The End of Certainty*, 1992, p. 59.

23   "scientific management": John Nethercote, "Australian public administration in perspective", APS Commission occasional paper.

24   "the Department": The Auditor-General, *Commonwealth Estate Property Sales – Department of Finance and Administration*, Audit Report No. 4, 2001–2002 Performance Audit, Commonwealth of Australia, 2001.

28–9 "famously warned": Gary Banks, *Evidence-based policy making: What is it? How do we get it?* ANU Public Lecture Series, presented by ANZSOG, Canberra, February 2009.

29–30 "The history of megaprojects": Malcolm Turnbull, speech to the AFR Infrastructure Summit, 11 June 2015.

31   "more challenging and interesting work": See: Alan Mitchell, "Time to end outsourcing and rebuild the public service", *Australian Financial Review*, 14 June 2015.

32   "so that there": Korda Mentha Forensic, National Disability Insurance Agency, Review of Board Requirements, December 2014.

33–4 "Aboriginal Industry": Noel Pearson, "Remote Control: Ten years of struggle and success in indigenous Australia", *Monthly*, May 2015.

34   "blind spots", "excessive focus" and "internal and external": Department of Health, *Capability Review*, Commonwealth of Australia, October 2014.

35   "now faces" and "*The Canberra Times*": Noel Towell, "Department faces biggest APS executive exodus in three decades", *Canberra Times*, 23 July 2015.

37   "So only about": Verona Burgess, "Well-functioning Australian government a distant memory for most public servants", *Australian Financial Review*, 19 August 2015.

39–40 "It is clear" and "We need a": Malcolm Turnbull, Doorstop interview, Canberra, 14 September 2015.

40   "fixed by a": *Economist*, "Stabbed in the Front", 19 September 2015.

43   "They do politics" and "All that there": David Marr, *Faction Man*, Quarterly Essay 59, September 2015, p. 44.

46–7 "public servants understood" and "Both politicians and": R.A.W. Rhodes and Anne Tiernan, *The Gatekeepers: Lessons from Prime Ministers' Chiefs of Staff*, Melbourne University Publishing, 2014.

48   "John Howard used to": Michael Thawley, to ACT division of Institute of Public Administration Australia inaugural annual conference, 23 September 2015.

48–9 "It can be": Don Russell, *Reflections on My Time in Canberra*, Crawford School lecture, 31 March 2014.

49   "Most of us": Thawley, 23 September 2015.

53–4 "The old class-bound lines": *Economist*, "Stabbed in the Front", 19 September 2015.

57   "Historians have tended" and subsequent quotes: Orlando Figes, *The Crimean War: A History*, Metropolitan Books, 2012.

60–2 "all these disparate" and subsequent quotes: Matt Bai, *All the Truth is Out: The Week Politics went Tabloid*, Alfred A. Knopf, 2014.

72   "There's no single": Malcolm Turnbull, quoted in Phillip Thomson, "Prime Minister Malcolm Turnbull: Don't turn Australian into a glorified mail box", *Canberra Times*, 23 September 2015.

73   "As at 1 July 2011": Martin Lumb, *The 43rd Parliament: Traits and Trends*, research paper, 2 October 2013.

74   "Rapid turnover of" and subsequent quotes: Clare O'Neil and Tim Watts, *Two Futures: Australia at a Critical Moment*, Text Publishing, 2015.

75   "polls asking": For example, Roy Morgan Image of Professions Survey 2015.

76–7 "main repositories" and subsequent quotes: Ron Ashkenas, "How to preserve institutional knowledge," *Harvard Business Review*, 5 March 2013.

78   "the size of" and subsequent quotes: John Faulkner, "Surveillance, intelligence and accountability: An Australian story".

80   "We're not just here": Thawley, 23 September 2015.

80–1 "The wise": Russell, 31 March 2014.

Michael Bachelard

Journalists unlucky enough to have spent a portion of our careers covering Labor factional politics are familiar with the dilemma David Marr faced when writing his excellent primer on Bill Shorten's rise.

The dilemma is that, though fascinating to insiders, the grindings of Labor's factional machine – at once impenetrable, distasteful and apparently crucial – are to outside observers dull to the point of stupor. But without understanding and accounting for the networks of influence and patronage that bind the union bosses, the branches (more accurately, the branch-stackers), the ethnic warlords and the parliamentarians, there is no explaining the Labor Party and how it identifies and promotes talent.

As Marr elegantly points out, Shorten's rise through this system was both ruthless and relentless. In a series of ever more complex deals in 2005, he bent the Victorian party and all its parts to his will so as to feed his capacious ambition. It was no small undertaking.

As I remember his pre-selection – and I covered it closely for the *Australian* – he was at once the party's most adept and most insecure manipulator. Almost everything he asked for, he got, but he still wanted more. Shorten wanted to make doubly, triply sure that he would gain pre-selection for his chosen safe seat, and then win it. The demands and deals he made in service of this ambition led to a cascade of other consequences that put several people out of their jobs and consumed the party for months, at both state and federal level. His ambition was not the only one being served by the massive ructions that shook the party that year, but somewhere in every local battle was Shorten, looking out for interests that invariably pointed back to himself. It didn't seem so at the time, but in retrospect this was a huge, virtually unprecedented disruption to the Victorian Labor Party.

Thanks to Tony Abbott and Dyson Heydon's royal commission, we now know that factional numbers were not the only component of Shorten's campaign. He was also raising funds by the tens of thousands of dollars or more, often from the employers he was simultaneously negotiating deals with. At least some of that money was directly used for his election campaign – particularly in the case of a campaign director funded by Unibuilt.

Shorten's career has been defined by his collection and use of numbers, whether it be to secure his own seat, to turf first Kevin Rudd, then Julia Gillard, out of the Lodge, or to secure the party's leadership from Anthony Albanese by sewing up the votes at the central level in the 2013 leadership contest after losing the popular ballot.

Otto von Bismarck famously compared sausage-making and law-making, saying that in neither case did we want to see the method of manufacture. It's unlikely he had in mind the neighbourhood snag-fest that goes along with voting in Australia, but his analogy holds true here as well: it does not pay to look too closely at the constituent parts of what we're biting into on election day – either literally or figuratively.

Bill Shorten is the very embodiment of the Bismarckian conundrum. He's a presentable leader emerging from an unpalatable process. He's steeped in factional manipulation, but still carries something of an air of innocence about him. His number-crunching, the deals he's made with the worst elements of his party's machine, have at times represented the height of cynicism. But as Labor's disabilities spokesperson, he was genuinely moved by the plight of the people he met, and was capable of turning that emotion into action, helping to craft the National Disability Insurance Scheme that will secure them a better deal.

Now Shorten has manoeuvred his way to being one step away from the prime ministership. A very big step nevertheless remains. Malcolm Turnbull presents a more significant challenge than Tony Abbott did – it's a pity that the timing of Marr's essay denied us his views on that head-to-head contest.

Shorten, meanwhile, has yet to attain mass political popularity. Perhaps that's another result of his conundrum: nobody sees him as being particularly tough. It's ironic that, for all the acuity and ruthlessness of Shorten's rise through Labor, the perception that he's not tough enough might prove to be his downfall. As Marr puts it: "He still wears the face his mother gave him, the face of a boy who wants to be liked. It's a charming mask that hides too much for his own good. This man would be more respected if, like Hawke, Keating and Howard, he let us see the bastard that's in there. Instead, the rough edges are politely hidden."

One example of this perception issue is that in the narrative surrounding Tony Abbott's fall, Shorten is not widely credited with the scalp – as Abbott was when he took down Turnbull, then Rudd (twice) and Gillard. Abbott himself, driven by his many flaws, is his own fourth victim, they say.

What all this means for Australian electoral politics it's still a little too soon to say. Malcolm Turnbull's rise has turned the spotlight back on Shorten, and not in a flattering way. The *Age* illustrator John Spooner depicted the Labor leader as a sitting duck, a large target painted on his downy chest, a gormless look about his beak. But Turnbull is just at the start of his honeymoon. That will inevitably sour. And as many a factional enemy has discovered over the years, it does not pay to underestimate Bill Shorten. His ability to do the numbers and his drive to power are profound. Marr has found a way, without once stupefying us, to remind us of that, and to suggest that we should not write off William Richard Shorten just yet.

Michael Bachelard

Rachel Nolan

David Marr writes that Bill Shorten has no great ambition for reform. His goal is power for Labor and Bill Shorten, "and decent administration for Australia." The trouble is that Labor can't win like that. That Labor has to have an agenda, that it relies for its electability, not only on its integrity, but also on its capacity to inspire hope, is a pearl of political wisdom passed on to me many years ago by a more experienced political friend. That wise friend later became a federal MP; perhaps ironically, he was the one vote who went across with Shorten in the belated decision to become a party to the knifing of Gillard as prime minister.

Marr writes that while Shorten believes in plenty of things – the Labor values of jobs, prosperity, education and health – there's nothing particularly distinctive in his standpoints, nothing brave. To defeat Malcolm Turnbull, Shorten will have to do better than that. He will have to move beyond being a safe pair of hands and take a giant leap of policy substance, as well as style. He will have to present an economic vision to the country – one that gives Australians the confidence to believe we can make it in a competitive, more Asian world. He'll also need new ideas for social reform, ideas that are truly Labor and run deeper than Turnbull's patrician smile.

For Shorten, as for Labor leaders before him, that journey begins very close to home, with the project of defining not just who he is, but what modern Labor is. In the week Marr's essay was published, headlines about the Labor Party were already ablaze. The Royal Commission had moved to Queensland, where reports suggested it had uncovered a classic union rort. Heydon's team grilled David Hanna, the former secretary of the Builders Labourers Federation, the allegation being that Mirvac had funded $150,000 worth of trades work on Hanna's new house. And while Hanna's defence was simply that he and the bosses were "good blokes," the implication was inescapable: that in paying off the union boss, the company had bought industrial peace.

The alleged rorting was not systemic – and so it was not Royal Commission gold – but the backstory was a classic one of union money in the ALP. While never a huge player, Dave Hanna had for some years wielded influence in the Queensland party. His deal-making approach – backed by employers' money, it now seems – had created discomfort and ultimately a split in the centre Labor Unity faction. When Hanna and his supporters moved the remains of the faction to the Left, they helped to deliver power to that side of the party for the first time in many years. And while the shift brought money and stability to a then very weak ALP, the quid pro quo was a conservative, almost frozen economic policy, a leash that if not deftly handled will tightly constrain the new Labor government.

Union membership has plummeted from nearly 45 per cent in the early 1990s to between 15 and 20 per cent now, but union power in politics, particularly Labor politics, has seen less of a diminution than a change. Unions bring less moral authority and less ability to mobilise than they did in the old days, but with super funds, training levies and the ability to get their hands on employers' cash, unions exert their influence through the chequebook. We know money talks.

The solution to this for Shorten will be a complex one. Simply to end union affiliation, as some shallow commentary suggests, would destabilise the party, change its historical nature and see the money flow to the Greens. There remains a critical role for unions in the workplace and the ALP, but their power must be diminished in keeping with their plummeting workforce coverage and they cannot be allowed to put a brake on the party's longstanding mission to modernise the country's economic base.

The great Labor leaders of the past have redefined the relationship between the party and its essential power base: Whitlam stared down the faceless men, then set about tariff cuts; Hawke changed the game with the Accord; and Keating won the battle of ideas outright on the need for economic reform. While it's sometimes forgotten in the eulogising of the past, all came from the Right. All brought Labor well away from the comforts of economic protection by promoting a vision of Australia as free-trading, educated, innovative and open to the world.

This challenge will in some respects be harder for Shorten than it was for Labor leaders before him – he has won his position not on the power of his ideas, but on his ability to negotiate and the fact that he is well-regarded inside the party. To present a new economic vision, he will have to step outside his comfort zone and burn some of the allies who have brought him this far. In politics, we are defined by our fights. If Shorten is to win, he must be more than Marr's "faction man." Taking on the unions is a hard fight, but one that Shorten must have.

Rachel Nolan

Race Mathews

David Marr's Quarterly Essay on Bill Shorten is strong in many respects. Marr shows Shorten to have sound Labor roots and values and to have done good policy work in areas such as establishing the National Disability Insurance Scheme and navigating workplace relations and the future of financial advice reform, but the essay perhaps underplays the corresponding obligation of ALP leaders to pass on the party in as good or better shape than they have found it.

The acid test of Shorten's leadership will be to achieve both an early return of the ALP to office and a comprehensive reform and renewal of the party. As Gough Whitlam told a hostile Victorian State Conference in 1967:

> We cannot convincingly oppose the conservatism of our political opponents with a conservatism of our own; we cannot stand as a Party of change when we fear change in our own structure. We cannot expect the people to trust us with the great decision-making processes of this nation when we parade, by retaining an exclusive and unrepresentative Party structure, our manifest distrust of our own rank and file within the decision-making processes of the Party.

At the time of the party's first ever election for its federal parliamentary leader, both Shorten and Anthony Albanese showed that they were alert to this obligation.

In Shorten's response to a questionnaire from the 'Local Labor' party reform and renewal group, he gave a number of undertakings to initiate both rules changes to democratise the party and hands-on measures to gain, retain and involve members through improved support for party branches and an upgrading of the membership experience. His response to the questionnaire reads in part:

- **Access:** It not always possible for members with family and work commitments, or for members in remote and country areas, to attend monthly Branch commitments. We must investigate and trial ways to offer alternative forms of branch organisation and involvement beyond the constraints of geography. We must find ways to use online platforms to help members engage. This could be connecting through virtual meetings or having the option of virtual branches when and where required, and for our rules to formalise this.

- **Organisation:** In line with better induction and training offerings to members, the Party should also develop simple online training modules for those elected to Branch Officer roles. This will help Branch Officers to be fully supported to develop the skills to run effective branches and to engage branch members. I would encourage ALP members with backgrounds in workplace education and training to assist the Party develop these modules.

- **Knowledge Sharing:** There should be the opportunity to report and apply successful Branch initiatives or learn from thriving Branches so we can continuously improve our operation and engagement. All Branches can benefit from hearing the success of our Branches and I want us to build a new organisational culture around celebrating and applying this success.

- **Community Connected:** We must make sure that Branches are properly connected to their communities and actively engage in locally-based progressive campaigns and activities. This should occur not just at elections but between elections. We must build on and sustain the successful work of our federal election fieldwork campaigns but focus on regular community engagement activities and campaigns between elections.

A signal democratisation success achieved at his instigation has been the adoption by the party's recent national conference of a landmark rules change to allow some 150 of the delegates to future conferences to be elected directly by and from rank-and-file party members. A near miss on his part was the failure of the conference to bring to a vote an intended measure for greater rank-and-file participation in pre-selections.

Less encouraging has been lack of progress towards fulfilment of his branch and member support pledges by the party's state administrations. Seemingly, his behind-the-scenes advocacy of the pledges has as yet fallen on deaf ears, and needs to become much more upfront and assertive in the face of those within the party who are most resistant to reform. State and territory branches must take responsibility for their failings and live up to the federal leader's vision.

Nor is that all. Rampant factional disregard for the party's rules, as exemplified by branch-stacking and the rorting of the requirement for secret ballots in pre-selections and election of party office-holders, has yet to be stamped out. The vexed question of relations between the party's rank-and-file members and its union affiliates, and the mutual misunderstandings and suspicions to which they needlessly give rise, remains unaddressed. For want of action on these fronts, many of the 15,000 new members who flocked to the party following the leadership contest or in protest against the excesses of the Abbott government are being lost to it. The challenge is to retain these newcomers by improving the quality of the membership experience and building up the capacity of branches and office-holders.

What our troubled times require is the reinvention of the party as it once was – the cutting political edge of a wider social movement that includes grassroots members, unions, communities and community groups on an equal footing. History will honour – and the electorate reward – the leader who accomplishes this.

Race Mathews

John Warhurst

Opposition leader Bill Shorten has had many critics during his two years in the job. Now that Malcolm Turnbull has become prime minister, quite a few of them think he has lost any chance of winning the next election. It should be remembered, however, that the polls are still evenly balanced and Turnbull has yet to strut his stuff in any meaningful way.

So Shorten should still be the subject of the sort of scrutiny that David Marr, the master of prime ministerial profiles, has given him in *Faction Man*. Marr is appalled by Shorten's path to power through the union movement, the Labor Party and the factions, for what it reveals about the modus operandi of these organisations. But he is still somewhat taken with Shorten's talents.

Nevertheless, he doubts that Shorten is up to the job and concludes with a stinging judgment, *pace* Daniel Andrews, that without doubt "he might have made a fine premier of Victoria." Shorten, according to Marr, is a limited man who has not yet shown that he can "scale up" from his successes in union and internal party politics.

All of the various knocks on Shorten are examined in the essay. Some of them are formulaic, including that no first-term Labor Opposition leader after the party has lost office has ever become prime minister. Though I note that both Andrews and Annastacia Palaszczuk in Queensland have recently done so at the state level, so perhaps the political environment is changing.

Other criticisms are substantial, including that he is excessively self-interested. Shorten is perceived to lack passion and dynamism and not to stand for anything. He is said to lack popular appeal, as shown by his failure to win the membership vote when he defeated Antony Albanese in the Labor leadership ballot. He is also dogged by his role in the two Labor leadership coups in 2010 and 2013 (perhaps that will diminish given Turnbull's own coup). The polls reflect his unpopularity, which was surpassed only by the unpopularity of Tony Abbott.

Overall he is seen not to be a sufficiently interesting man, suffering by comparison with successful Labor Opposition leaders Gough Whitlam, Bob Hawke and Kevin Rudd. There is something in this point, but perhaps it is misplaced. Governments lose elections, Oppositions don't win them.

Let's not forget that many said the same thing of John Howard, who made a virtue of his so-called ordinariness and went on to be Australia's second-longest-serving prime minister. Perhaps Australia has a Messiah complex if it always needs titans for its political leaders.

Marr concludes with what can be seen as either a savage put-down or damning with faint praise: "His goal is power for Labor and Bill Shorten, and decent administration for Australia." Decent administration is generally seen as the province of state governments, but after recent turmoil, perhaps national-level voters might just settle for it.

Faction Man could easily have been called "Union Man" or "Victorian Labor Man," given its focus. Marr has the ability to piece together and clearly explain complex matters like union and factional politics. And the picture he paints is a very unattractive one, in which Shorten fully participated, of shifting alliances and backstabbing, all with the narrow goal of a seat in federal, state or municipal politics. To put it mildly, it is an unedifying read and helps to explain why both sides of major party politics are on the nose with voters.

As with Rudd, Abbott and Turnbull, the story of this aspiring political leader has a Catholic twist. There has already been far too much generalised commentary about Catholic values and, in particular, Jesuit values as they apply to political life in this country. Wisely, Marr eschews too much of this. But he does tell a powerful story of the role of Shorten's impressive and much-loved mother, Ann McGrath, in shaping her son and insisting that he have a Jesuit education. That education, Marr says, left Shorten with an "undogmatic faith" and important business connections of the type a GPS school can provide. Marr also does his bit to break down the frequent shallow generalisations about a Jesuit education by speculating on the differences between Riverview, which Abbott attended, and Xavier, Shorten's school, at this time. There are many different types of Jesuits, and it would not be surprising if each of their schools had a distinct culture.

John Warhurst

This piece first appeared in *Eureka Street* on 4 October 2015.

Frank Bongiorno

Most of us feel we don't know Bill Shorten all that well. Thanks to David Marr's excellent Quarterly Essay, we are now entitled to feel we know him better. Still, there are aspects of Shorten's career that seem to me only comprehensible once its context is taken more fully into account. In particular, the post-1983 transformation of the union movement and the ALP are critical in understanding the kind of politician that he is, but they have so far received limited public attention.

Shorten is a Generation-Xer, one of that group who now increasingly compose Australia's political elite. We have only had one such prime minister, Julia Gillard, but she was born in 1961, often considered its cusp. Born in 1967, the year the Beatles gave us *Sgt. Pepper's Lonely Hearts Club Band*, Shorten sits squarely within this group. As such, his experiences are of a type shared with other members of that generation. These go beyond a possible partiality to power ballads and John Hughes films. He was a teenager and university student in the 1980s, a period when Labor dominated national politics under the prime ministership of Bob Hawke and also had considerable electoral success in the states – including in Shorten's own Victoria, where John Cain Junior led the first Labor government in thirty years. Marr writes of Shorten and his friends watching federal Labor's 1983 victory on television and finding inspiration in Hawke. It would be surprising if a teenager such as Shorten, contemplating a political career, had not found in the new Labor prime minister an inspiration, and Hawke has surely been a powerful model for Shorten's career.

But only up to a point. Hawke became a national figure on the back of an immensely powerful public persona, and of his role first as an Australian Council of Trade Unions (ACTU) advocate in the 1960s, and then as its president during the turbulent 1970s. Shorten also chose a career in the union movement, but in the Australian Workers Union (AWU). By comparison with Hawke's, his opportunities for cutting a figure on the national stage before he entered parliament were meagre, although he did so with considerable ingenuity during the Beaconsfield mining disaster of 2006. Marr also points out that whereas Hawke tended to get his lieutenants to line up the numbers for him, Shorten has been more active in looking after his own. Yet for all his gifts of persuasion and organisation, Shorten has never given any indication of possessing the kind of public charisma Hawke had in spades.

But there is a more critical difference, and one which has nothing to do with the respective personalities of the two men. When Hawke came to office in 1983, almost half the workforce were still union members; by the time Shorten was beginning to make his mark as an AWU man in the 1990s, this figure had dropped to about 35 per cent. Today, it is well under 20 per cent.

There are complex reasons for this decline. It owes something to the changing nature of the workforce – the shift away from manufacturing and towards service industries, and the rise of part-time and casual labour – but also a great deal to policy: notably, the effective end of compulsory unionism in most workplaces as a result of legislation passed under conservative state governments, such as that of Jeff Kennett in Victoria. Other critical changes of the early 1990s also drastically shifted the nature of the Australian union movement: union amalgamations, the rise of enterprise bargaining and the development of a system of compulsory superannuation in which unions were participants through the industry super funds.

It was in this new union environment that Shorten became a leading figure, with the added spice that he chose a branch of a union – the Victorian AWU – that had been so grossly mismanaged by some of its officials, and was so riven by internal conflict, that its continued existence could not be taken for granted. The AWU was also under pressure elsewhere: for instance, in Western Australia's Pilbara, where employer aggression from the time of the Robe River dispute of 1986–87 had, by the 1990s, essentially eradicated the union from the workplace.

It is not hard to see how Shorten's qualities and skills would have found their mark in this environment. The combination of casualisation and repression of the union movement at the hands of state governments, leading to the end of closed-shop unionism, meant that the unions now needed to work much harder to recruit and then keep their members than had been the case under the old arbitration system. These circumstances provided an opening for skilled organisers, and Shorten filled it very well. Some of the ways in which he drew members into the AWU's circle have raised eyebrows, including those of Dyson

Heydon, but it is easy to see why arrangements in which employers paid the union fees of their workers would have been attractive to the organisation during this period.

Added to this, however, was the rise of enterprise bargaining. It is easy today to overlook just how significant this was as a departure from previous patterns of industrial relations. These had, of course, often included collective bargaining, but in a very different regulatory environment, one in which state intervention through courts, boards, commissions and tribunals had played a much more influential role in setting wages and conditions through the award system.

Enterprise bargaining meant that a large blue-collar union such as the AWU was involved in literally hundreds of agreements with employers. Securing "the deal" became more central to the way unions operated, and each union dealt with employers, often face-to-face, in an environment in which they were frequently competing with rival organisations for the allegiance of members. In the case of the AWU, its rivalry with the militant Construction, Forestry, Mining and Energy Union was a key factor. But perhaps of equal importance was the way that enterprise bargaining resulted in new kinds of direct relationships between union officials and individual employers. So, in a different way, did the involvement of union officials in industry super funds.

This is quite different from the environment of what Gerard Henderson called the old "industrial relations club," where Bob Hawke forged friendships with corporate bosses or the leaders of peak organisations – the likes of Peter Abeles and George Polites – that, from 1983, carried over into his corporate style of government, with its economic and tax summits, its Economic Planning Advisory Council and the like. Yes, Shorten's relationship with the late Richard Pratt has some of the hallmarks of Hawke's business mateships, but the more systemic relations with business-owners and managers that the AWU built up in the process of striking enterprise bargaining agreements appear to have been more significant.

All of this has had substantial implications for the Labor Party. These were perhaps not fully foreseen in the early 1990s, but a most revealing internal party review from the period, headed by the then national secretary, Bob Hogg, pointed to some of the dangers. "The decline in union coverage of the total workforce and the number of unions affiliated to the Party as well as the current [union] amalgamation and restructuring" all had "very serious implications for the Party," the review concluded. "Those implications are serious in terms of the Party remaining representative and in terms of its internal organisational power structures . . . As unions become such a substantial prize in the ALP then political considerations will become the dominant factor in union elections rather than the industrial considerations and the broader interests of the union membership."

Indeed: and the snake-pit of factional Labor Party politics in Victoria, which David Marr describes so vividly, is one very direct outcome. With the decline of both the branch rank-and-file ALP membership and union coverage, factional bosses such as Shorten, Stephen Conroy and Kim Carr often seem more like princes of the states of the Holy Roman Empire at the time of the Thirty Years' War than factional leaders of the Hawke–Keating era, efficiently dividing among their charges the spoils of office. This also helps us to make sense of Shorten's decision, as an ambitious up-and-comer, to make his way through the AWU – with its control of all those votes on the floor of Labor Party conferences (and therefore, ultimately, of party offices and pre-selections) – rather than take the ACTU route chosen by Hawke decades earlier.

Marr makes the valid point that, despite its many faults, the turbulent Victorian branch of the ALP produces very talented politicians – of whom Shorten is a prime example. But Marr also poses the important question: can Shorten scale up to the tasks required of a national leader? A number of senior Labor politicians since Paul Keating, while competent (or better) as ministers and shadow ministers, have failed to shine as party leaders or prime ministers. Each has appeared to have some of the qualities and skills needed for the job, but not the full complement. Beazley, Crean, Latham, Rudd and Gillard: the list is already long. Is it growing?

Frank Bongiorno

David Marr

We were making good time through the mountains at the head of the Manning Valley when the radio cut to Malcolm Turnbull in Canberra. Reception was terrible. Through bursts of static Turnbull could be heard taking his leader apart. He was not making Julia Gillard's mistake. Nothing was wrapped in euphemism. We sat in the car in Walcha fielding calls from the ABC and listening to the challenge unfold. And all I could think was: what about my Quarterly Essay?

I've had the ground shift under an essay before. My 2010 attempt to explain the strange ways of Kevin Rudd had been in the shops for only a few weeks when a message reached me in London to say the prime minister was gone. That essay was read as an explanation for Labor's sudden decision to push Rudd out the window. Sales were strong. But the triumph of Turnbull in September meant one of the chief reasons to be curious about Bill Shorten vanished. I had written *Faction Man* with this question in mind: how could such a leader take the recently thrashed Labor Party back to power? In the opening pages of the essay I'd remarked that a "hard rule of the last half-century has been that only larger-than-life leaders bring Labor in from Opposition. Whitlam, Hawke and Rudd were such men. Shorten isn't." And I'd added: "But neither is Abbott." Say what you like about the new prime minister, Turnbull is larger-than-life.

The trucks were backed up to the warehouse the afternoon of the leadership challenge to take 23,000 copies of *Faction Man* to the nation. We halted the trucks for a couple of days before deciding to press ahead: only a few paragraphs at the top and bottom of the 100-page text addressed the contest between Shorten and Abbott. The political landscape had changed, but not my subject: *Faction Man* is about Bill Shorten. In a press release I spruiked the essay as an extended examination of the strengths and weaknesses of the Labor leader as he faces a new and more formidable opponent. "He is not to be dismissed. A hidden man in so many ways, Bill Shorten remains a contender."

I'm not so sure now of that verdict. Only a month has passed but Australian politics has been transformed. Abbott's time in office seems so far away that children might be studying it in school. His devoted followers are dealing with their grief for the most part behind closed doors. Only Andrew Bolt is still mourning in the Murdoch tabloids. Voters have forgotten the man who didn't make much impression as leader of the Opposition: wordy Malcolm, arrogant Malcolm and silly Malcolm. Instead they see a figure in whom they can invest their best hopes: a big, intelligent man free of Abbott's un-Australian horror of the future. They told pollsters immediately they preferred Turnbull to Shorten as their prime minister, and overwhelmingly so. But for a while Australians remained sceptical of his government, even a government where a woman ran the armed forces. Too much had gone wrong, it seemed, to be too easily forgiven. While that lasted, Shorten was still a strong contender. But the mood shifted. By mid-October, he was standing on the wrong side of a crevasse opening up between Labor and the Coalition.

He began to pump out policies. The Year of Ideas he promised for 2015 began as the year was drawing to an end. He became more combative. His tone darkened. In all this he was at his most impressive since winning the leadership. But as he lifted his game, his shortcomings became more apparent. He's tough and he's a clever strategist and he's used to winning. But against Turnbull he seems a little figure. That may not be fair. Turnbull's frailties as well as his strengths have yet to be tested in office. Anything can happen between now and the uncertain date at which Australia will go to an election. But Bill Shorten, after twenty years in the unions and the factions and a mere seven in parliament, doesn't seem to be built to take the weight of the nation on his shoulders.

David Marr

19 October 2015

Michael Bachelard is investigations editor at the *Age* and was Indonesia correspondent for the three years to January 2015. He is an award-winning reporter and the author of two books, the most recent being *Behind the Exclusive Brethren*.

Frank Bongiorno is the author of *The Eighties: The Decade that Transformed Australia* and *The Sex Lives of Australians: A History* and a regular contributor to *Inside Story*. He teaches history at the Australian National University.

David Marr has written for the *Sydney Morning Herald*, the *Age*, the *Saturday Paper* and the *Monthly*, been editor of the *National Times*, a reporter for *Four Corners*, presenter of ABC TV's *Media Watch* and now writes for the *Guardian*. His books include *Patrick White: A Life*, *The High Price of Heaven*, *Dark Victory* (with Marian Wilkinson), *Panic* and five Quarterly Essays.

Race Mathews is a former principal private secretary and resident policy wonk for Gough Whitlam, a federal MP, state MP and minister and academic.

Rachel Nolan was the state member for Ipswich in the Queensland parliament from 2001 to 2012. She held the portfolios of Transport, Natural Resources, Finance and the Arts as part of Anna Bligh's Labor government.

Laura Tingle is political editor of the *Australian Financial Review*. She won the Paul Lyneham Award for Excellence in Press Gallery Journalism in 2004, and Walkley awards in 2005 and 2011. She is the author of *Chasing the Future: Recession, Recovery and the New Politics in Australia*. Her previous Quarterly Essay was the acclaimed *Great Expectations*.

John Warhurst is emeritus professor of political science at the Australian National University and a *Canberra Times* columnist.

QUARTERLY ESSAY DIGITAL SUBSCRIPTIONS NOW AVAILABLE SUBSCRIBE to Quarterly Essay & SAVE up to 25% on the cover price

Enjoy free home delivery of the print edition and full digital access on the Quarterly Essay website, iPad, iPhone and Android apps.

Subscriptions: Receive a discount and never miss an issue. Mailed direct to your door.

- ☐ **1 year print and digital subscription** (4 issues): $79.95 within Australia. Outside Australia $119.95
- ☐ **1 year print and digital gift subscription** (4 issues): $79.95 within Australia. Outside Australia $119.95
- ☐ **2 year print and digital subscription** (8 issues): $129.95 within Australia
- ☐ **2 year print and digital gift subscription** (8 issues): $129.95 within Australia
- ☐ **1 year digital only subscription** (4 issues): $39.95
- ☐ **1 year digital only gift subscription** (4 issues): $39.95

All prices include GST, postage and handling

Plese turn over for subscription order form, or subscribe online at **www.quarterlyessay.com**
Alternatively, call 1800 077 514 or 03 9486 0288, fax 03 9486 0244 or email subscribe@blackincbooks.com

Back Issues: (Prices include GST, postage and handling.)

- [ ] **QE 1** ($15.99) Robert Manne *In Denial*
- [ ] **QE 2** ($15.99) John Birmingham *Appeasing Jakarta*
- [ ] **QE 3** ($15.99) Guy Rundle *The Opportunist*
- [ ] **QE 4** ($15.99) Don Watson *Rabbit Syndrome*
- [ ] **QE 6** ($15.99) John Button *Beyond Belief*
- [ ] **QE 7** ($15.99) John Martinkus *Paradise Betrayed*
- [ ] **QE 8** ($15.99) Amanda Lohrey *Groundswell*
- [ ] **QE 9** ($15.99) Tim Flannery *Beautiful Lies*
- [ ] **QE 10** ($15.99) Gideon Haigh *Bad Company*
- [ ] **QE 11** ($15.99) Germaine Greer *Whitefella Jump Up*
- [ ] **QE 12** ($15.99) David Malouf *Made in England*
- [ ] **QE 13** ($15.99) Robert Manne with David Corlett *Sending Them Home*
- [ ] **QE 14** ($15.99) Paul McGeough *Mission Impossible*
- [ ] **QE 15** ($15.99) Margaret Simons *Latham's World*
- [ ] **QE 16** ($15.99) Raimond Gaita *Breach of Trust*
- [ ] **QE 17** ($15.99) John Hirst *"Kangaroo Court"*
- [ ] **QE 18** ($15.99) Gail Bell *The Worried Well*
- [ ] **QE 19** ($15.99) Judith Brett *Relaxed & Comfortable*
- [ ] **QE 20** ($15.99) John Birmingham *A Time for War*
- [ ] **QE 21** ($15.99) Clive Hamilton *What's Left?*
- [ ] **QE 22** ($15.99) Amanda Lohrey *Voting for Jesus*
- [ ] **QE 23** ($15.99) Inga Clendinnen *The History Question*
- [ ] **QE 24** ($15.99) Robyn Davidson *No Fixed Address*
- [ ] **QE 25** ($15.99) Peter Hartcher *Bipolar Nation*
- [ ] **QE 26** ($15.99) David Marr *His Master's Voice*
- [ ] **QE 27** ($15.99) Ian Lowe *Reaction Time*
- [ ] **QE 28** ($15.99) Judith Brett *Exit Right*
- [ ] **QE 29** ($15.99) Anne Manne *Love & Money*
- [ ] **QE 30** ($15.99) Paul Toohey *Last Drinks*
- [ ] **QE 31** ($15.99) Tim Flannery *Now or Never*
- [ ] **QE 32** ($15.99) Kate Jennings *American Revolution*
- [ ] **QE 33** ($15.99) Guy Pearse *Quarry Vision*
- [ ] **QE 34** ($15.99) Annabel Crabb *Stop at Nothing*
- [ ] **QE 35** ($15.99) Noel Pearson *Radical Hope*
- [ ] **QE 36** ($15.99) Mungo MacCallum *Australian Story*
- [ ] **QE 37** ($15.99) Waleed Aly *What's Right?*
- [ ] **QE 38** ($15.99) David Marr *Power Trip*
- [ ] **QE 39** ($15.99) Hugh White *Power Shift*
- [ ] **QE 40** ($15.99) George Megalogenis *Trivial Pursuit*
- [ ] **QE 41** ($15.99) David Malouf *The Happy Life*
- [ ] **QE 42** ($15.99) Judith Brett *Fair Share*
- [ ] **QE 43** ($15.99) Robert Manne *Bad News*
- [ ] **QE 44** ($15.99) Andrew Charlton *Man-Made World*
- [ ] **QE 45** ($15.99) Anna Krien *Us and Them*
- [ ] **QE 46** ($15.99) Laura Tingle *Great Expectations*
- [ ] **QE 47** ($15.99) David Marr *Political Animal*
- [ ] **QE 48** ($15.99) Tim Flannery *After the Future*
- [ ] **QE 49** ($15.99) Mark Latham *Not Dead Yet*
- [ ] **QE 50** ($15.99) Anna Goldsworthy *Unfinished Business*
- [ ] **QE 51** ($15.99) David Marr *The Prince*
- [ ] **QE 52** ($15.99) Linda Jaivin *Found in Translation*
- [ ] **QE 53** ($15.99) Paul Toohey *That Sinking Feeling*
- [ ] **QE 54** ($15.99) Andrew Charlton *Dragon's Tail*
- [ ] **QE 55** ($15.99) Noel Pearson *A Rightful Place*
- [ ] **QE 56** ($15.99) Guy Rundle *Clivosaurus*
- [ ] **QE 57** ($19.99) Karen Hitchcock *Dear Life*
- [ ] **QE 58** ($19.99) David Kilcullen *Blood Year*
- [ ] **QE 59** ($22.99) David Marr *Faction Man*

Payment Details: I enclose a cheque/money order made out to Schwartz Publishing Pty Ltd. Please debit my credit card (Mastercard or Visa accepted).

Card No. ☐☐☐☐ ☐☐☐☐ ☐☐☐☐ ☐☐☐☐

Expiry date /   **CCV**   **Amount $**

Cardholder's name   **Signature**

Name

Address

Email   **Phone**

Post or fax this form to: Quarterly Essay, Reply Paid 90094, Carlton VIC 3053 / Freecall: 1800 077 514
Tel: (03) 9486 0288 / Fax: (03) 9486 0244 / Email: subscribe@blackincbooks.com
Subscribe online at **www.quarterlyessay.com**